DEFINING MOMENTS
THE HARLEM RENAISSANCE

DEFINING MOMENTS
THE HARLEM RENAISSANCE

Kevin Hillstrom

P.O. Box 31-1640
Detroit, MI 48231

Omnigraphics, Inc.

Cherie D. Abbey, *Managing Editor*

Peter E. Ruffner, *Publisher*
Matthew P. Barbour, *Senior Vice President*

Elizabeth Collins, *Research and
Permissions Coordinator*
Kevin M. Hayes, *Operations Manager*

Allison A. Beckett and Mary Butler, *Research Staff*
Cherry Stockdale, *Permissions Assistant*
Shirley Amore, Martha Johns, and Kirk Kauffman,
Administrative Staff

Copyright © 2008 Omnigraphics, Inc.
ISBN 978-0-7808-1027-3

Library of Congress Cataloging-in-Publication Data

Hillstrom, Kevin, 1963-
  The Harlem Renaissance / Kevin Hillstrom.
    p. cm. -- (Defining moments)
  Includes bibliographical references and index.
  Summary: "Provides a detailed, factual account of the emergence and development of the Harlem
Renaissance and its ongoing effect on American society. Features include a narrative overview, bio-
graphical profiles, primary source documents, detailed chronology, glossary, and annotated sources
for further study"--Provided by publisher.
  ISBN 978-0-7808-1027-3 (hardcover : alk. paper) 1. Harlem Renaissance. 2. African American
arts--New York (State)--New York--20th century. I. Title.
  NX512.3.A35H55 2008
  810.9'896073--dc22
                                                                              2007051132

The information in this publication was compiled from the sources cited and from other sources considered reliable.
Additional copyright information can be found on the photograph credits page of this book. While every possible effort
has been made to ensure reliability, the publisher will not assume liability for damages caused by inaccuracies in the data,
and makes no warranty, express or implied, on the accuracy of the information contained herein.

This book is printed on acid-free paper meeting the ANSI Z39.48 Standard. The infinity symbol that appears above indi-
cates that the paper in this book meets that standard.

Printed in the United States

TABLE OF CONTENTS

PRIMARY SOURCES

PREFACE

Throughout the course of America's existence, its people, culture, and institutions have been periodically challenged—and in many cases transformed—by profound historical events. Some of these momentous events, such as women's suffrage, the civil rights movement, and U.S. involvement in World War II, invigorated the nation and strengthened American confidence and capabilities. Others, such as the McCarthy era, the Vietnam War, and Watergate, have prompted troubled assessments and heated debates about the country's core beliefs and character.

Some of these defining moments in American history were years or even decades in the making. The Harlem Renaissance and the New Deal, for example, unfurled over the span of several years, while the American labor movement and the Cold War evolved over the course of decades. Other defining moments, such as the Cuban missile crisis and the terrorist attacks of September 11, 2001, transpired over a matter of days or weeks.

But although significant differences exist among these events in terms of their duration and their place in the timeline of American history, all share the same basic characteristic: they transformed the United States' political, cultural, and social landscape for future generations of Americans.

Taking heed of this fundamental reality, American citizens, schools, and other institutions are increasingly emphasizing the importance of understanding our nation's history. Omnigraphics' *Defining Moments* series was created for the express purpose of meeting this growing appetite for authoritative, useful historical resources. This series, which focuses on the most pivotal events in U.S. history from the twentieth century forward, will be of enduring value to anyone interested in learning more about America's past—and in understanding how those historical events continue to reverberate in the twenty-first century.

Each individual volume of *Defining Moments* provides a valuable resource for readers interested in learning about the most profound events in our nation's history. Each volume is organized into three distinct sections—Narrative Overview, Biographies, and Primary Sources.

- The **Narrative Overview** provides readers with a detailed, factual account of the origins and progression of the "defining moment" being examined. It also explores the event's lasting impact on America's political and cultural landscape.

- The **Biographies** section provides valuable biographical background on leading figures associated with the event in question. Each biography concludes with a list of sources for further information on the profiled individual.

- The **Primary Sources** section collects a wide variety of pertinent primary source materials from the era under discussion, including official documents, papers and resolutions, letters, oral histories, memoirs, editorials, and other important works.

Individually, each of these sections is a valuable resource for users. Together, they comprise an authoritative, balanced, and absorbing examination of some of the most significant events in U.S. history.

Other notable features contained within each volume in the series include a glossary of important individuals, places, and terms; a detailed chronology featuring page references to relevant sections of the narrative; an annotated bibliography of sources for further study; an extensive general bibliography that reflects the wide range of historical sources consulted by the author; and a subject index.

Acknowledgements

This series was developed in consultation with a distinguished Advisory Board comprising public librarians, school librarians, and educators. They evaluated the series as it developed, and their comments and suggestions were invaluable throughout the production process. Any errors in this and other volumes in the series are ours alone. Following is a list of board members who contributed to the *Defining Moments* series:

Gail Beaver, M.A., M.A.L.S.
Adjunct Lecturer, University of Michigan
Ann Arbor, MI

Melissa C. Bergin, L.M.S., NBCT
Library Media Specialist
Niskayuna High School
Niskayuna, NY

Rose Davenport, M.S.L.S., Ed.Specialist
Library Media Specialist
Pershing High School Library
Detroit, MI

Karen Imarisio, A.M.L.S.
Assistant Head of Adult Services
Bloomfield Twp. Public Library
Bloomfield Hills, MI

Nancy Larsen, M.L.S., M.S. Ed.
Library Media Specialist
Clarkston High School
Clarkston, MI

Marilyn Mast, M.I.L.S.
Kingswood Campus Librarian
Cranbrook Kingswood Upper School
Bloomfield Hills, MI

Rosemary Orlando, M.L.I.S.
Library Director
St. Clair Shores Public Library
St. Clair Shores, MI

Comments and Suggestions

We welcome your comments on *Defining Moments: The Harlem Renaissance* and suggestions for other events in U.S. history that warrant treatment in the *Defining Moments* series. Correspondence should be addressed to:

Editor, *Defining Moments*
Omnigraphics, Inc.
P.O. Box 31-1640
Detroit, MI 48231-1640
E-mail: editorial@omnigraphics.com

HOW TO USE THIS BOOK

Defining Moments: The Harlem Renaissance provides users with a detailed and authoritative overview of this event, as well as the principal figures involved in this pivotal episode in U.S. history. The preparation and arrangement of this volume—and all other books in the *Defining Moments* series—reflect an emphasis on providing a thorough and objective account of events that shaped our nation, presented in an easy-to-use reference work.

Defining Moments: The Harlem Renaissance is divided into three primary sections. The first of these sections, the **Narrative Overview**, provides a detailed, factual account of the emergence and development of the Harlem Renaissance. It explores the factors that transformed Harlem into the "capital of black America" in the 1920s, explains how civil rights activism of the early twentieth century made the Renaissance possible, and discusses the myriad ways in which African-American literature, art, and music illuminated black culture and changed the course of American race relations.

The second section, **Biographies**, provides valuable biographical background on leading figures involved in the movement, including the proud and fiery civil rights philosopher W.E.B. Du Bois, controversial actor and singer Paul Robeson, jazz legend Duke Ellington, and Langston Hughes, the "poet laureate" of the Harlem Renaissance. Each biography concludes with a list of sources for further information on the profiled individual.

The third section, **Primary Sources**, collects essential and illuminating documents from the Harlem Renaissance. This collection includes Langston Hughes's famous manifesto of artistic independence, "The Negro Artist and the Racial Mountain"; dancer Frankie Manning's recollections of the glamorous Savoy Ballroom; Alain Locke's influential and insightful essay "Enter the New Negro," and a selection of poems penned by some of the Harlem Renaissance's leading literary voices.

Other valuable features in *Defining Moments: The Harlem Renaissance* include the following:

- Attribution and referencing of primary sources and other quoted material to help guide users to other valuable historical research resources.
- Glossary of Important People, Places, and Terms.
- Detailed Chronology of events with a *see reference* feature. Under this arrangement, events listed in the chronology include a reference to page numbers within the Narrative Overview wherein users can find additional information on the event in question.
- Photographs of the leading figures and major events associated with the Harlem Renaissance.
- Sources for Further Study, an annotated list of noteworthy works about the movement.
- Extensive bibliography of works consulted in the creation of this book, including books, periodicals, Internet sites, and videotape materials.
- A Subject Index.

NARRATIVE OVERVIEW

PROLOGUE

The Harlem Renaissance ranks as one of the most pivotal and influential eras in American history. It marked the emergence of African Americans into the mainstream of the nation's art, music, literature, and culture while simultaneously proclaiming the unique vitality and character of the African-American experience. But although they are in agreement about its cultural importance, Renaissance scholars offer varying opinions about virtually every other aspect of this movement. Even the years in which the Harlem Renaissance took place are in dispute. Some historians date the origins of the Harlem Renaissance to the 1910s, when Harlem first emerged as a population and cultural center for black Americans, and cite the ugly Harlem riots of 1935 as the close of the era. Other scholars, however, insist that the Harlem Renaissance was almost exclusively an event of the 1920s. They claim that the Renaissance first flowered immediately after World War I, when America was roiled by economic and social upheaval, and that it came crashing down in 1929, when the nation's worst-ever stock market crash ushered in the Great Depression.

Some scholars even prefer to use the term "Negro Renaissance" instead of Harlem Renaissance. They acknowledge that Harlem was the center of African-American cultural and political growth in the 1920s and 1930s, but they point out that cities like New Orleans, Atlanta, Washington, D.C., and Chicago also harbored important black musicians, artists, writers, and intellectuals during these same decades.

Historians also differ in their perspectives on the long-term legacy of the Harlem Renaissance. Their debate mirrors the one waged by the men and women most closely associated with the Harlem Renaissance, both during the Renaissance's greatest heights and long after the movement passed. Looking back, some members of the movement grimly concluded that the Harlem

Renaissance failed to decisively improve black-white relations in America, as many had hoped it would. Still others proclaimed that they never held out much hope that the Renaissance would usher in a new and more harmonious era of U.S. race relations or lift black Americans out of their inferior position in American society. Instead, they simply expressed satisfaction about creating art and literature that reflected commitment to their artistic vision and pride in their racial heritage.

Other giants of the Harlem Renaissance, however, claimed that the movement's turbulent blend of political rhetoric, civil rights activism, musical excitement, and literary milestones laid the groundwork for a better life for future generations of African Americans. They asserted that the art and literature of the Harlem Renaissance forced white Americans to finally take notice of "Negro" life, and that these works gave blacks a vital infusion of pride and self-confidence. Many scholars agree, claiming that the major civil rights gains of the 1950s and 1960s might never have occurred without the Renaissance.

One of the most eloquent spokesmen for African Americans during the Harlem Renaissance was novelist and civil rights activist James Weldon Johnson. Writing in "Race Prejudice and the Negro Artist," an essay that appeared in the November 1928 issue of Harper's, Johnson left no doubt about his impressions of the movement's impact. He firmly proclaimed his belief that the Harlem Renaissance was forever changing American racial attitudes—and America itself—for the better:

> . . . There is a common, widespread, and persistent stereotyped idea regarding the Negro, and it is that he is here only to receive; to be shaped into something new and unquestionably better. The common idea is that the Negro reached America intellectually, culturally, and morally empty, and that he is here to be filled—filled with morality, filled with culture. In a word, the stereotype is that the Negro is nothing more than a beggar at the gate of the nation, waiting to be thrown crumbs of civilization.
>
> Through his artistic efforts the Negro is smashing this immemorial stereotype faster than he has ever done through any other method he has been able to use. He is making it realized that he is the possessor of a wealth of natural endowments and that he has long been a generous giver to America. He is impressing upon the national mind the conviction that he is an active and

important force in American life; that he is a creator as well as a creature; that he has given as well as received; that he is the potential giver of larger and richer contributions.

In this way the Negro . . . has placed himself in an entirely new light before the American people. I do not think it too much to say that through artistic achievement the Negro has found a means of getting at the very core of the prejudice against him by challenging the Nordic superiority complex. A great deal has been accomplished in this decade of "renaissance." Enough has been accomplished to make it seem almost amazing when we realize that there are less than twenty-five Negro artists who have more or less national recognition; and that it is they who have chiefly done the work.

Those words were written more than three-quarters of a century ago, at the peak of the Harlem Renaissance. Now it is up to modern-day Americans to decide whether Johnson's proud and hopeful words about the impact of the Renaissance were justified.

Chapter One

BLACK AMERICA
AFTER SLAVERY

We refuse to allow the impression to remain that the Negro-American assents to inferiority, is submissive under oppression and apologetic before insults. Through helplessness we may submit, but the voice of protest of ten million Americans must never cease to assail the ears of their fellows, so long as America is unjust.

—from the Niagara Movement's
"Declaration of Principles," 1905

The American Civil War, which raged across the United States from 1861 to 1865, brought the nation's long and shameful era of slavery to a close. President Abraham Lincoln's Emancipation Proclamation of 1863 dealt a death blow to the practice of slavery in the American South. After the Confederacy formally surrendered to federal forces in the spring of 1865, it seemed to countless African Americans that a new age of freedom and opportunity was finally at hand.

These hopes were further bolstered by the early stages of Reconstruction, a twelve-year period (1865-1877) after the war when the federal government forced Southern states to end a variety of discriminatory practices against blacks. During these years, Republican lawmakers in the North used their political muscle to pass two major amendments to the U.S. Constitution. The Fourteenth Amendment granted citizenship and various civil rights to blacks, and the Fifteenth Amendment guaranteed black voting rights. As a condition of readmittance into the Union, Southern states also were required to form new state governments and revise their state constitutions to accommodate black civil and economic rights.

As a result of these changes, black school principals, legislators, and mayors appeared in the South for the first time, and African Americans even represented several Southern states in the U.S. Congress. In addition, Reconstruction brought about the creation of the first statewide public school systems in the South, the founding of the first black institutions of higher learning, and a wave of black land ownership.

The End of Reconstruction

Even as these gains were being made, however, toxic levels of white racism and post-Civil War bitterness pounded away at the foundations of Reconstruction. The violent white supremacist organization known as the Ku Klux Klan spread like wildfire across the American South during the Reconstruction years, and countless other white Southerners complained bitterly about the swift rise of blacks from slavery to citizenship. "Slavery disappeared much faster than the race prejudice which had grown up with it," summarized historian Allen W. Trelease in *Reconstruction: The Great Experiment*. "The firm conviction that God had created black men as an inferior race—possibly for the very purpose of serving white men—did not die so easily."

During the 1870s white Southern planters, mill owners, and legislators orchestrated a backlash against the laws and principles of Reconstruction. Their efforts received broad support from other whites in the South. Equally importantly, federal authorities showed dwindling enthusiasm for preserving black civil rights gains. This retreat came about in large measure because many Northerners were weary of more than a decade of violence and strife in the South. Another factor was that the cities of the North were grappling with serious problems of their own. "Northern whites had a hard time sustaining interest in the fate of freedmen with their own world shaken by economic depression, political corruption, and violent class conflict, all bitter by-products of the North's industrialization," wrote historian Kevin Boyle in *Arc of Justice*. As a result, some Northern lawmakers signaled that they were willing to sacrifice black civil rights in return for a measure of peace and stability in the South.

By 1876 Reconstruction was teetering on the edge of collapse. During the previous few years, Southern state legislatures had imposed "Black Codes" that stripped black citizens of virtually all of their hard-won civil rights. Incidents of violence and terrorism against blacks increased in numerous sections of the South. State and municipal governments were systematically purged of black members as well.

The final blow to Reconstruction was the presidential election of November 1876, when neither Republican candidate Rutherford B. Hayes (the lopsided choice of Northern voters) nor Democratic nominee Samuel J. Tilden (the overwhelming preference of white Southerners) garnered enough electoral votes to claim victory. After weeks of bitter political wrangling, Democrats agreed to recognize Hayes as the nineteenth president of the United States—in return for a guarantee that he would remove all federal troops charged with enforcing civil rights laws from the South. After his inauguration in March 1877, Hayes fulfilled his part of the bargain. Federal troops were ordered out of the South. This development left black Americans at the mercy of a white population that, with few exceptions, was determined to re-establish white dominance over all of the region's economic, social, and political levers of power.

Exploitation and Desperation

Over the next two decades, many Southern blacks became trapped in lives that were frighteningly similar to those endured by their enslaved ancestors. All across the region, state legislatures passed "Jim Crow" laws that codified segregation and discrimination against African Americans in virtually every area of their daily existence. With most avenues of economic advancement closed to them, black families in the South turned to sharecropping, an agricultural system in which black farmers (and poor white farmers) lived and grew crops on white-owned land. In exchange, the landowners received half of the crop—usually cotton—raised by each family. This arrangement, combined with the high interest rates that white planters charged sharecropping families for seeds, tools, and other essentials, kept most sharecroppers in a state of perpetual economic dependency and poverty.

The daily struggle to survive also made it difficult for black families to absorb the loss of labor when children were in school, so rates of illiteracy remained high among black Southerners. Black youths who did receive a formal education attended schools that were markedly inferior to those of white students. This chasm became even greater after the U.S. Supreme Court's notorious *Plessy v. Ferguson* ruling of 1896. This ruling, which came on the heels of several other Court decisions that chipped away at black civil rights, formally sanctioned state laws that segregated schools, restrooms, parks, residential neighborhoods, railroad cars, and other public facilities. Although the facilities were technically required to be "separate but equal," white legisla-

A white planter in Mississippi stands among African-American sharecropping families.

tors in the South diverted almost all public funding to white-only schools and neighborhoods, leaving black community members with virtually nothing.

Encouraged by their progress in reversing the Reconstruction-era civil rights gains of blacks, white Southerners pressed their advantage. "They piled prohibition on prohibition," wrote Boyle in *Arc of Justice:*

> Blacks couldn't be buried in the same cemeteries as whites. They couldn't eat in the same restaurant. They couldn't ride in the front of city streetcars. They couldn't drink from the same drinking fountains. Whites also segregated their workplaces. Blacks could be servants and farm laborers, of course, and they could work in the turpentine and lumber camps, where most whites didn't want to go. But whites claimed the vast majority of jobs for themselves. They also demanded privileges that superiority conferred. They expected blacks to step off the sidewalk when a white person approached. They insisted that blacks keep their eyes downcast when they spoke to whites. . . .

They felt free to level any insult, to inflict any injury, without fear of reprisal. Jim Crow taught the great mass of southern whites to see ordinary places and everyday interactions as sacred and to protect the sacred by embracing the profane.

Reign of Terror

The hardships endured by Southern blacks worsened in other ways as well during the last two decades of the nineteenth century. Racist theories of black inferiority, many of them cloaked in a veneer of "scientific" reasoning, became widely accepted in both the South and North. These theories enabled proponents to rid themselves of any sense that they were morally obliged to improve the grim conditions under which most African Americans lived. Whites told themselves that blacks were impoverished and uneducated because of innate shortcomings, not because American laws and societal conditions were stacked against them.

Black Americans also lived each day under a threatening shadow of racial violence. Countless black men in the South dared not exercise their constitutional right to vote out of fear that they or their families would be terrorized or even killed by whites. Most black Southerners took pains to be submissive or at least accommodating in their interactions with whites in order to minimize their risk of persecution. Nonetheless, by the early 1890s local Ku Klux Klan groups or loosely organized white mobs lynched an average 150 Southern blacks each year. Race riots also broke out periodically in towns and cities all across the South. These explosions of white-on-black violence not only resulted in the deaths of black men, women, and children, but the destruction of black homes, businesses, and property. Few black people had the economic resources to recover from such vandalism. Moreover, race riots and lynchings had a brutal effect on African-American psyches, for they underscored how vulnerable blacks were to the mood of the surrounding white community. Given all of these factors, it is little wonder that African Americans in the rural South became convinced that racial justice and economic opportunity would always be beyond their grasp.

The Great Northern Migration

In the early years of the twentieth century, many black Southerners responded to the grim landscape of the South by turning their gaze to the

This illustration from a 1920 issue of *The Crisis* symbolizes how lynching in Southern states provided powerful motivation for African Americans to immigrate to the North.

North. Sick of living in fear and poverty, they decided to leave their homeland behind and seek out new and better lives in New York City, Cleveland, Chicago, Detroit, Philadelphia, and other industrial cities of the North. Most African American individuals and families who took part in this exodus from the South reasoned that they had nothing to lose. "As long as Jim Crow ruled the South, that system of segregation, subordination, and terror created powerful incentives for leaving and staying away," wrote James N. Gregory in *The Southern Diaspora.*

But the blacks who fled the South in the opening years of the new century were not only running *away* from a land of heartache and injustice, but also running *toward* a region that held at least the possibility of a happier and more fulfilling existence. "From the days of slavery," pointed out historian Cary Wintz in *Black Culture and the Harlem Renaissance,* "the North had held a special position in the mythology of Southern blacks as a place of refuge where equality and racial justice abounded." The North was also the home of a small but growing number of African-American intellectuals and activists such as W.E.B. Du Bois, who seemed to be able to issue calls for racial justice without fear of assassination or imprisonment (see Du Bois biography, p. 103).

"As long as Jim Crow ruled the South, that system of segregation, subordination, and terror created powerful incentives for leaving and staying away," wrote James N. Gregory in **The Southern Diaspora.**

Finally, black Southerners were intrigued by the contents of Northern-based black-owned newspapers that filtered down into the South. Advertisements in the Chicago *Defender,* the *Afro-American* (Baltimore), the *New York Age* and other black papers all trumpeted the need for factory workers—especially after the onset of World War I, when Northern industrial firms armed with lucrative wartime contracts actively recruited Southern blacks to fill the labor gap left by a dramatic downturn in European emigration. As the nations of Europe filled their military ranks with men who might otherwise have sailed to America, black American men and women rushed northward to make the most of this perceived economic opportunity.

The first stirrings of the great migration of rural Southern blacks to the industrial cities of the North (and the metropolitan centers of the South, to a lesser degree) became detectable as early as the 1890s. As late as 1910, however, U.S. Census Bureau figures indicate that 90 percent of the nation's black population remained in the South. It was not until 1915 that the mass migration of blacks northward began in earnest. Over the next fifteen years the number of blacks living in New York City soared from fewer than 92,000 to nearly 328,000. Other industrial centers such as Chicago, Cleveland, and Detroit registered even greater increases in their rate of black population growth.

New arrivals to the industrial centers of the North, however, often found the environment to be a hostile one. Discrimination against black Americans was commonplace in Northern school systems, restaurants, theatres, and hotels—even though most Northern states had civil rights laws in place that made many of these discriminatory practices illegal. Many labor unions were unwilling to admit black members either, so black men and women from the South were left with unskilled jobs that paid low wages. Black community leaders appealed to the federal government for help in addressing these brazen violations of American law, but their pleas were brushed aside or stonily ignored. This situation remained unchanged until World War I, when the resulting labor shortages opened rail yards, steel mills, and other factory doors to blacks.

Some Northern cities and towns in the early twentieth century even suffered from the same ugly spasms of racial violence that afflicted so many Southern communities during that same time. White gangs of hooligans and white supremacist groups constituted a genuine threat to the physical safety of blacks in some communities, and full-fledged race riots erupted in cities ranging from New York to Springfield, Illinois, in the early 1900s. Remarkably, however, living conditions in the North still represented an improvement over those in the Jim Crow South, so few black Americans who took part in the great migration to the Northern "Promised Land" ever went back.

The entrance of the United States into World War I in 1917 further intensified racial tensions in America. Most blacks supported the war effort, and thousands of black men rushed to join the armed forces to defend their country, even though that country had treated them so badly for so long—and even though the U.S. military adhered to the same segregationist policies that had brought them such misery over the years. Even black champions of racial justice and integration such as Du Bois urged African-American men to set aside their qualms and take up arms on behalf of the United States. Black communities hoped that by displaying their love of country, they could persuade white America to reconsider its racist attitudes and laws.

As the war went on, black troops proved their mettle in battle after battle. Black soldiers, however, found that their patriotism and sacrifices seemed

"A Philosophy in Time of War"

When the United States entered World War I in 1917, some African Americans objected to the thought of seeing black men marching off to war. They reasoned that blacks did not owe their country any military service, given the hostility and discriminatory treatment they endured on a daily basis from their countrymen and their government. But many other African Americans argued that whatever its faults, the United States was still home and still worth defending. W.E.B. Du Bois summarized this viewpoint in "A Philosophy in Time of War," which was published in the August 1918 issue of *Crisis*. In this article, Du Bois asserted that:

> First, This Is Our Country.
>
> We have worked for it, we have suffered for it, we have fought for it; we have made its music, we have tinged its ideals, its poetry, its religion, its dreams; we have reached in this land our highest modern development and nothing, humanly speaking, can prevent us from eventually reaching here the full stature of our manhood. Our country is at war. The war is critical, dangerous and worldwide. If this is OUR country, then this is OUR war. We must fight it with every ounce of blood and treasure.

to have little impact on the racist attitudes of their white countrymen. Black soldiers were harassed in the communities surrounding training bases in the South, and those who were deployed in Europe were routinely subjected to discriminatory treatment. Even non-military service organizations like the Federal Council of Churches and the YMCA practiced discrimination in doling out benefits and attention to white and black units. These injustices were further highlighted by the warm and respectful treatment that black troops received in France. Black soldiers were quick to recognize the contrast between the attitudes of most French citizens and those of their white countrymen, and their resentment about the racial inequities in American society surged dramatically as a result.

Back at home, meanwhile, racial violence continued to make a mockery of stated American principles of equality. As black American soldiers fought

Members of the Harlem-based 369th Regiment return home to New York after fighting in World War I.

and died in Europe, 3,000 white Tennesseans responded to a local newspaper's invitation to watch a "live Negro" be killed by burning. To the west, a rampaging white mob in East St. Louis killed forty African Americans in response to a local factory's decision to hire black workers. The murder victims included a two-year-old child who was shot and then tossed into a burning building.

The Red Summer of 1919

After the United States and its allies emerged victorious from World War I in the spring of 1919, white and black American soldiers were welcomed home to their respective neighborhoods with joyful celebrations. But even though white and black American soldiers had endured the crucible of war together (albeit in segregated units), their shared experiences did not produce any improvements in U.S. race relations. To the contrary, the sudden demobilization of working-age men greatly increased the competition for industrial jobs and allowed companies to pay lower wages to working men. These developments infuriated white workers in the North, many of whom placed the blame for the downturn in their economic fortunes squarely on the shoulders of black immigrants from the South.

African Americans, however, suffered the most from the postwar labor glut. As white military veterans returned home and the flow of immigrants from Europe to the United States resumed, thousands of hardworking blacks were dumped back onto the unemployment line simply because of the color of their skin. The postwar labor pool became so deep that even unskilled jobs became off-limits to blacks in many instances. The famous Harlem Renaissance writer Langston Hughes recalled in his autobiography, *The Big Sea,* that when he arrived in New York City in 1922 as a young man, "I bought the papers and began to answer ads regarding jobs I thought I could handle—office boy, clerk, waiter, bus boy, and other simple occupations. Nine times out of ten—*ten* times out of ten, to be truthful—the employer would look at me, shake his head and say, with an air of amazement: 'But I didn't advertise for a colored boy.'"

Surging unemployment rates and sinking wages were not the only events that tempered American jubilation about the end of the war. Controversy also simmered around other issues, including the growing militancy of the women's suffrage movement, proposals to enact sweeping prohibition laws, bitter clashes between corporate management and workers over unionization and working conditions in a host of industries, and increasingly frantic warnings about "Negro Invasions" of rural blacks into American cities.

Many white Americans felt confused and angry about the controversies and uncertainties swirling around them. To numerous white families, the cumulative uproar over these issues seemed to threaten the stability of their homes, neighborhoods, and communities. Many of these white men and women looked for someone to blame for the social and economic convulsions that were wracking America, and they quickly settled on blacks—the most convenient and vulnerable targets in their range of vision.

During the summer and fall of 1919, race riots exploded in more than twenty cities across the United States. In virtually every case, the riots were triggered by white mobs that attacked black men, women, and children at random and without any provocation. Some of the cities scarred by these riots were in the North, and Chicago actually suffered the worst rioting of any American city. Over the course of thirteen days, the Chicago riot took the lives of thirty-eight citizens (twenty-three blacks and fifteen whites). The riots also injured another 537 people, and left an estimated 1,000 black families homeless. Other cities blasted by race riots included Washington, D.C., Charleston, South Carolina, and Knoxville, Tennessee. In Phillips County, Arkansas, hundreds of white men spent three days and nights stalking down every black man, woman, and child they could find. When the violence finally subsided, the official body count of blacks killed was twenty-five. Some members of the traumatized black community, however, claimed that as many as 200 blacks had been slain, their bodies dumped in desolate woods, in remote cane fields, or in the muddy waters of the Mississippi River.

> *"[The black man] must be willing to die fighting when he is right!" wrote the editors of Harlem's Amsterdam News. "When police authorities fail to protect him and his family; when courts of law desert him; when his own government fails to take a stand in his behalf, he faces death anyway, and might just as well die fighting!"*

The race riots of 1919 came to be widely known as the Red Summer, in recognition of the African-American blood that was shed during those months of terror. The victims of this mayhem included women, children, the elderly, and black men who only a few weeks before had been serving their country in Europe. But scholars note that the Red Summer was unlike previous race riots that had afflicted America in one important respect: in Chicago, Washington, D.C., and several other towns and cities, blacks dared to fight back against the white mobs, inflicting casualties of their own.

Many of the black men who took up arms were proud, battle-hardened World War I veterans, and it was their example that inspired other blacks to strike back against their tormentors. In several instances native-born blacks were joined by recent immigrants from the West Indies, many of whom expressed anger and disillusionment about the poisonous levels of racial hostility that existed in their newly adopted country. This previously unseen black militancy stunned white America. The *New York Times*, for example, complained afterward that "there had been no trouble with the Negro before the war, when most admitted the superiority of the white race."

This defiance did not dissipate, either. From 1919 forward, black newspapers and periodicals displayed a greater willingness to sanction armed defense as a legitimate response to the threat of white violence. "[The Negro] must face death if he is to live!" wrote the editors of Harlem's *Amsterdam News* in 1925. "He must be willing to die fighting when he is right! When police authorities fail to protect him and his family; when courts of law desert him; when his own government fails to take a stand in his behalf, he faces death anyway, and might just as well die fighting!"

A New Era of Black Leadership

Black actions of self-defense during the Red Summer also reflected major changes in the ways that African-Americans thought about themselves and their rightful place in America. During the first two decades of the twentieth century, black intellectual leaders had declared feelings of racial pride—and

Booker T. Washington was the most prominent black spokesman in America at the turn of the century.

impatience with racial injustice—in voices of steadily rising strength and conviction. They interpreted the events of Red Summer as clear evidence that the time had come to attack racial discrimination and build a new and healthier model of race relations.

Back in the late nineteenth century, the most visible leader of the African-American community had been Booker T. Washington. An educator and founder of the Tuskegee Institute, a vocational school for blacks, Washington championed a philosophy of racial advancement that emphasized economic growth and self-sufficiency—even if it meant continued discrimination and inequities in other areas, like education and civil rights. Washington's conciliatory approach, his humble demeanor, and his limited agenda made him an unthreatening figure to white power brokers, many of whom expressed support for his program of "mutual progress."

By the end of the nineteenth century, however, several influential black intellectuals had publicly broken ranks with Washington and his philosophy of

W.E.B. Du Bois stood at the forefront of a new generation of black leaders in the early twentieth century.

racial accommodation. Angry and frustrated by the continued marginalization of blacks to the fringes of American society, men such as Monroe Trotter, John Hope, and Du Bois declared that blacks should insist on equal educational opportunities and work to end discrimination, segregation, and racial violence throughout the country (see "W.E.B. Du Bois Discusses Black Hopes and

Booker T. Washington and the "Atlanta Compromise"

Booker T. Washington's status as a leading black spokesman—and his reputation as someone who was willing to delay civil rights gains for African Americans in return for greater economic security—was cemented in September 1895, when he delivered a famous speech before a mostly white audience at the Cotton States and International Exposition in Atlanta, Georgia. This "Atlanta Compromise" address, as it came to be known, was warmly received by Southern whites. They welcomed Washington's assurances that blacks were more interested in improving their economic circumstances than in challenging discrimination and segregation in the Jim Crow South. Following is a brief excerpt from Washington's speech:

> The wisest among my race understand that the agitation of questions of social equality is the extremest folly, and that progress in the enjoyment of all the privileges that will come to us must be the result of severe and constant struggle rather than of artificial forcing. No race that has anything to contribute to the markets of the world is long in any degree ostracized. It is important and right that all privileges of the law be ours, but it is vastly more important that we be prepared for the exercise of these privileges. The opportunity to earn a dollar in a factory just now is worth infinitely more than the opportunity to spend a dollar in an opera-house.

Sources:

Harlen, Louis R., ed. *The Booker T. Washington Papers,* Vol. 3. Urbana: University of Illinois Press, 1974.

Dreams," p. 157). According to Du Bois, the responsibility for realizing these goals lay with the "Talented Tenth," the minority of black Americans who had the educational and economic resources to lead *all* blacks to a better place in American society. Du Bois believed that the Talented Tenth would not only provide inspiration and leadership to the larger black community, but also shatter racial stereotypes held by bigoted whites. Their accomplishments would thus lay the foundation for a new age of racial harmony and social equality.

In 1905 the simmering divisions between these militant civil rights leaders and the "Bookerites"—supporters of Washington—exploded into the open. In July, Du Bois and Trotter gathered together more than two dozen black leaders on the Canadian side of Niagara Falls. This group, which came to be known as the Niagara Movement, produced a historic "Declaration of Principles" that proclaimed the innate dignity of the black race and attacked racial discrimination in American society.

The Niagara Movement failed to attract mass support, in large measure because of opposition from Washington and his allies, and it officially disbanded in 1911. But many of the Niagara Movement's leading figures, including Du Bois, were pivotal in founding a far more influential civil rights organization—the National Association for the Advancement of Colored People (NAACP)—in 1909. Indeed, the Niagara Movement is regarded as a forerunner of sorts to the NAACP. It also helped paved the way for the founding of another major civil rights group, the National Urban League (NUL), in 1910.

By the time that Washington died in 1915, Du Bois and his allies in the NAACP and NUL had replaced the founder of the so-called "Tuskegee Machine" as the most influential voices representing black America. "The Bookerites' sacrifice of civil rights for economic gain . . . lost its appeal not only to educated and enterprising African Americans but to many of those white philanthropists and public figures who had once solemnly commended it," observed historian David Levering Lewis. "The Talented Tenth formulated and propagated the new ideology being rapidly embraced by the physicians, dentists, educators, preachers, businesspeople, lawyers, and morticians comprising the bulk of the African-American affluent and influential—some 10,000 men and women, out of a total population in 1920 of more than 10 million."

By the early 1920s, many African-American men and women who had taken this new ideology of empowerment and equal rights to heart had become convinced that blacks—and the nation as a whole—stood on the brink of an exciting new era of social justice. "A good part of white America frequently asks the question, 'What shall we do with the Negro?'" wrote James Weldon Johnson, who served as general secretary of the NAACP throughout the 1920s. "In asking the question it completely ignores the fact that the Negro is doing something with himself, and also the equally important fact that the Negro all the while is doing something with America."

Chapter Two

BEGINNINGS OF THE HARLEM RENAISSANCE

So here we have Harlem—not merely a colony or a community or a settlement—not at all a "quarter" or a slum or a fringe—but a black city located in the heart of white Manhattan, and containing more Negroes to the square mile than any other spot on earth. It strikes the uninformed observer as a phenomenon, a miracle straight out of the skies.

—James Weldon Johnson in *Black Manhattan*

During the 1910s and 1920s, the so-called Talented Tenth—African-American men and women who were at the forefront of efforts to improve the lives of all black Americans—spoke with increasing frequency of the "New Negro." According to these black leaders, the New Negro rejected the racist stereotypes of the past and expressed pride in his/her ethnic heritage. The New Negro also demanded that the United States—the self-proclaimed land of freedom and democracy—end its discriminatory practices and give black Americans the civil liberties that were their birthright.

These activists and community leaders, although they were educated and primarily from the nation's small black middle-class, came from all walks of life and held many different views on an assortment of social and political issues. But they shared a genuine commitment to tearing down the discriminatory barriers that kept most African-American families on the lowest rungs of American society. In addition, they were united in their belief that African American culture and creativity needed to be nurtured and supported in ways that it had never been before. Finally, as historian Cary D. Wintz noted in *Remembering the Harlem Renaissance,* the leading black voices of the early

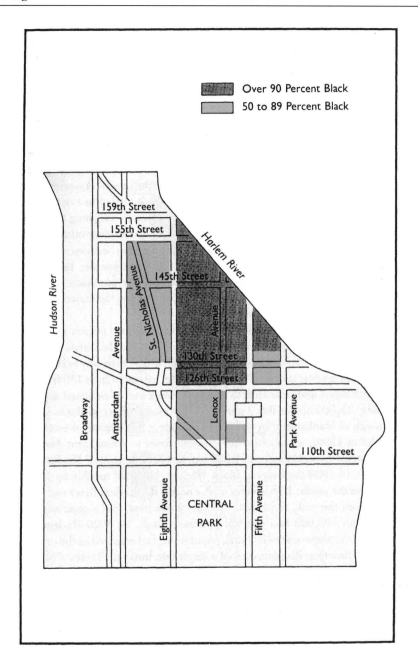

This map shows the African-American population in Harlem and wider Manhattan, 1900–1930. Maps on pages 24 and 25 are reprinted from Wintz, Cary D. *Black Culture and The Harlem Renaissance.* College Station: Texas A&M University Press, 1996. © Texas A&M University Press.

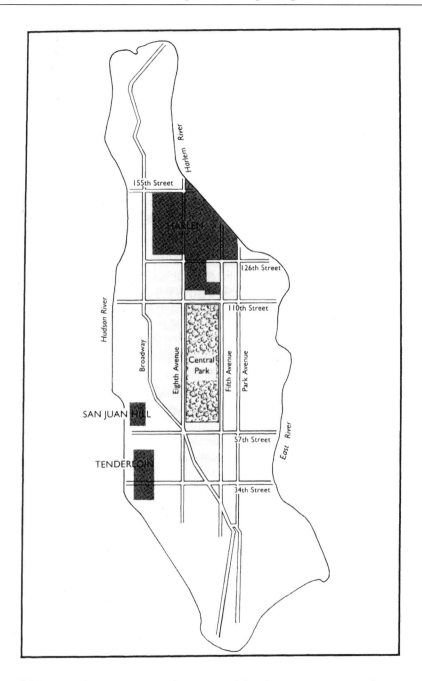

By 1930, African Americans in New York accounted for the great majority of residents in the neighborhoods of Harlem, San Juan Hill, and the Tenderloin.

twentieth century shared one other thing in common: they all, "to a greater or lesser degree, were connected to Harlem at the time that Harlem was emerging as the cultural, intellectual, and political center of black America."

The Capital of "Black America"

Harlem is a neighborhood perched on the northern edge of New York City, in the borough of Manhattan. In some ways Harlem was an unlikely candidate to become the unofficial capital of black America in the 1920s. As recently as 1900, Harlem had been an affluent white neighborhood that was home to many of the city's wealthier Jewish residents. Most black residents of the city at that time were located in Manhattan neighborhoods to the west, in slums known as San Juan Hill and the Tenderloin.

In the first years of the twentieth century, however, several trends converged to spark the rapid transformation of Harlem into a black community. During this period, a small—but symbolically important—number of successful black entrepreneurs and professionals used their savings to relocate their families from the ghettos of the Tenderloin and San Juan Hill to the outskirts of Harlem. In addition, black newcomers from the American South and the West Indies began pouring into New York City in numbers that were too great for traditional black neighborhoods to contain. Finally, Harlem's housing market, which had undergone a speculative construction boom in the 1890s, went into a sustained slump in the early 1900s. The depressed economic conditions left many of Harlem's houses and apartment properties empty at a time when Manhattan's black population was growing by leaps and bounds.

Black families first entered Harlem on its western and southern edges, but their expansion into the heart of the community was relatively swift. Black realtors who were eager to assist their fellow African Americans were one factor in this rapid transformation, but bigotry and fear were far more potent forces. When a black family moved onto a previously all-white block in Harlem, white families quickly moved out. "They felt that Negroes as neighbors not only lowered the values of their property, but also lowered their social status," explained James Weldon Johnson in *Black Manhattan*. "Seeing that they could not stop the movement, they began to flee. They took fright, they became panic-stricken, they ran amuck. Their conduct could be compared to that of a community in the Middle Ages fleeing before an epidemic of the black plague, except for the fact that here the reasons were not so sound. . . .

In 1917 more than 8,000 African Americans marched in downtown New York City to protest racial violence across the country.

The presence of a single coloured family in a block, regardless of the fact that they might be well-bred people, with sufficient means to buy their new home, was a signal for precipitate flight. The stampeded whites actually deserted house after house and block after block."

During the 1910s the transition of Harlem from a white community to a black one further accelerated. The "color line" dividing white and black Harlem moved steadily north and east, fed by continued black demand for decent housing and white hysteria about the "Negro invasion" of their neighborhoods. The perception that Harlem was becoming a black community was also bolstered by the growing public profile of Harlem-based civil rights organizations such as the National Urban League and the National Association for

Adam Clayton Powell Sr.
and the Harlem Abyssinian Baptist Church

Harlem churches were a major part of the spiritual and social lives of many African-American residents during the Harlem Renaissance. One of the most important of these religious institutions was the Abyssinian Baptist Church. Established in 1805, it ranks as one of the five oldest black Baptist churches in the United States. For the first century of its existence, the church was located in downtown New York City, but in 1923 senior pastor Adam Clayton Powell Sr. engineered its relocation to its present Harlem address on West 138th Street.

Powell ranks as one of the most influential and respected religious leaders in U.S. history. He was born in Franklin County, Virginia, on May 5, 1865, just as the Civil War was drawing to a close. After earning a theological degree from Wayland Seminary (now part of Virginia Union University) in 1892, he pastored at several churches in the northern United States. He took over as pastor of Abyssinian Baptist Church in 1908.

Over the course of his 29-year stint at the helm of the church, Powell proved himself to be a talented administrator, an inspiring religious leader, and a committed advocate for the Harlem community. Like a number of other African-American clergy in New York City during the Renaissance era,

the Advancement of Colored People. W.E.B. Du Bois, James Weldon Johnson, A. Philip Randolph, and other leading black intellectuals of the era also made their home in Harlem during these years. Finally, some of the earliest civil rights protests in American history took place in New York City during this time. In 1917, for example, Adam Clayton Powell Sr. and other Harlem religious leaders joined with the NAACP to organize a solemn parade in protest against a series of race riots and lynchings that had taken place across the country over the previous few weeks. More than 8,000 African Americans, most of them from Harlem, took place in this "Silent Protest" down New York's Fifth Avenue on July 28.

As a result of all these events, Harlem by 1920 had acquired an almost legendary reputation among African Americans from Birmingham to Boston.

Powell insisted that churches had a moral responsibility to treat social problems confronting the community. "Christianity is more than preaching, praying, singing and giving; it is all of these but a great deal more," wrote Powell in a 1923 essay for *Opportunity*. "The church will never draw and hold the masses by essays on faith, but by showing her faith by her works."

These beliefs led Powell to build one of the first community recreation centers in Harlem. In addition he established an ambitious slate of education and social ministry programs that operated out of the church. A founding member of the National Urban League, he also consistently preached a gospel of racial pride and self-respect. Powell retired in 1937, but he remained an active member of the Harlem community until his death in 1953. His successors—Adam Clayton Powell Jr. (his son, who also was the first African-American to represent the state of New York in the U.S. Congress), Samuel Dewitt Proctor, and Calvin O. Butts II—have all been prominent African-American spiritual leaders as well. Today, the Harlem Abyssinian Baptist Church remains one of the most influential political, social, and religious institutions in New York City.

Sources:

Gore, Robert. *We've Come This Far: The Abyssinian Baptist Church*. New York: Stewart, Tabori, and Chang, 2001.

Powell Sr., Adam Clayton. "The Church in Social Work." *Opportunity*, January 1923.

"Its name evoked a magic that lured all classes of blacks from all sections of the country to its streets," wrote historian Cary D. Wintz in *Black Culture and the Harlem Renaissance*. "Harlem became the race's cultural center and a Mecca for its aspiring young. . . . Harlem, in short, was where the action was in black America during the decade following World War I" (see "James Weldon Johnson Praises the People and Spirit of Harlem," p. 177).

The African-American women and men who descended on Harlem ranged enormously in their talents, ambitions, and moral character, as is the case with every community of any size. Some of Harlem's church leaders were dedicated to the spiritual and social betterment of the community; others were charlatans. Some of the residents were determined to support their families through honest labor; others were bootleggers and racketeers and prosti-

A black police officer provides directions to a black businessman in downtown Harlem, circa 1920.

tutes. Some were quiet, church-going folk; others routinely caroused late into the night. But whatever their differences, they all took enormous comfort in the fact that for the first time in American history, blacks had a thriving community that they could call their own. The famed entertainer Cab Calloway recalled that he was "awestruck by the whole scene" the first time he visited Harlem. "I had never seen so many Negroes in one place before in my life," he wrote in his autobiography *Of Minnie the Moocher and Me*.

Marcus Garvey and the "Back to Africa" Movement

Another exciting element of life in Harlem in the late 1910s and early 1920s was the meteoric rise and fall of Marcus Garvey, a Jamaican whose message of black nationalism and separatism took New York City by storm. As a young man, Garvey traveled widely throughout Jamaica and Central America. At most of his stops he witnessed disheartening examples of racial and economic exploitation of native peoples by British colonial authorities. By the time Garvey immigrated to the United States in 1916, he had developed a militant vision of worldwide black independence from white rule—and he was convinced that he was destined to take a leadership role in making this vision a reality.

In early 1917 Garvey settled in Harlem and set about building up his Universal Negro Improvement Association (UNIA), which he had founded back in Jamaica in 1914. Black pride and black economic self-sufficiency were the philosophical cornerstones of the UNIA, as Garvey himself proclaimed in an essay he titled "Africa for the Africans":

> [The UNIA] is organized for the absolute purpose of bettering our condition, industrially, commercially, socially, religiously and politically. We are organized not to hate other men, but to lift ourselves, and to demand respect of all humanity. We have a program that we believe to be righteous; we believe it to be just, and we have made up our minds to lay down ourselves on the altar of sacrifice for the realization of this great hope of ours, based upon the foundation of righteousness. We declare to the world that Africa must be free, that the entire Negro race must be emancipated from industrial bondage, peonage and serfdom; we make no compromise, we make no apology in this our declaration. We do not desire to create offense on the part of other races, but we are determined that we shall be heard, that we shall be given the rights to which we are entitled.

Unlike other black leaders who were calling for the dismantling of segregation in American society, Garvey embraced the idea of racial separatism. He told the thousands of blacks who crowded into Harlem's Liberty Hall for his weekly speeches that he intended to build a new nation-state in Africa populated with black American immigrants. "I have a vision of the future, and I see before me a picture of a redeemed Africa, with her dotted cities, with her beautiful civilization, with her millions of happy children, going to and fro," he declared in "Africa for the Africans." "Our program [is] the only solution

Marcus Garvey inspired an immensely popular black separatist movement in the late 1910s.

to the great race problem. There is no other way to avoid the threatening war of the races that is bound to engulf all mankind, which has been prophesied by the world's greatest thinkers; there is no better method than by apportioning every race to its own habitat."

Garvey's separatist beliefs alarmed Johnson, Du Bois, and other black leaders in Harlem, but the charismatic Jamaican electrified working men and women in New York City. "Short, squat, beaming with visions, regally attired, the visitor from Jamaica, in a spellbinding West Indian cadence, gave voice to dreams that literally blew the minds of a large segment of his impoverished generation of black humanity in the New World" recalled Renaissance writer Arna Bontemps in *The Awakening: A Memoir.*

By 1920 Garvey owned an enormously popular weekly newspaper, *The Negro World,* and had launched the Black Star Line, a steamship venture in which only black investors were permitted to own stock. In addition, nation-wide membership in Garvey's UNIA surpassed one million by the end of 1920. In the space of a few short years, Garvey had vaulted himself to the forefront of black leadership in the United States.

Over the next few years, though, Garvey's empire came crashing down. In 1922 he and three other Black Star Line officials were arrested for mail fraud. That same year, Garvey met with Ku Klux Klan leaders who declared their support for his scheme to solve America's racial problems by taking blacks back to Africa. When Randolph, Du Bois, and other promi-nent blacks in Harlem learned of this meeting, the reaction was instanta-neous and furious. Within a matter of days, the editors of the *Messenger,* an influential black periodical, issued a formal call to arms against the Jamaican: "We urge all ministers, editors, and lecturers who have the inter-ests of the race at heart to gird up their courage, put on new force, and pro-ceed with might and main to drive the menace of Garveyism out of this country." In 1923 Garvey was convicted of the mail fraud charges, and after he exhausted his appeals he was imprisoned. By 1927, when he was deported back to Jamaica, Garvey and the UNIA had lost much of their influence in the United States. He died in Europe thirteen years later after suffering a massive stroke.

Today, Garveyism is often viewed as a separate but parallel phenomenon of the Harlem Renaissance era. Many of Garvey's political objectives, for example, were strongly opposed by other leading black spokesmen more closely associated with the Renaissance. But in other respects Garvey helped build the environment that made the Harlem Renaissance possible. Much of the literature and art created during the Harlem Renaissance reflected Gar-vey's beliefs in ethnic pride and the common brotherhood of black people. His example inspired many black people in Harlem and elsewhere to become activists for social and political change.

The West Indian Immigrant in America

Black nationalist Marcus Garvey was the most famous emigrant from the West Indies in the early twentieth century, but he was but one of tens of thousands of other West Indians who immigrated to the United States in the 1910s and 1920s. In 1900, for example, fewer than 3,600 foreign-born blacks lived in Harlem, but by 1920 this population had grown to more than 36,000 foreign-born blacks. The great majority of these foreign-born immigrants were from the British West Indies.

Most black emigrants from the West Indies and other parts of the Caribbean left their native lands because of poverty, overcrowding, and devastating hurricanes and other natural disasters. Emigration to America was eased by the fact that many Caribbean nations and territories already shipped large quantities of fruit, sugar, and other goods to the United States on a regular basis. The existence of these reliable transportation networks made booking passage a fairly simple and inexpensive exercise.

Upon arriving in America, many West Indians were shocked at the level of discrimination and racial hatred that prevailed in many parts of the country. Unlike native-born blacks, who had been conditioned to react

Equality through Arts and Letters

Garvey's dramatic rise was only one of the reasons that the streets of Harlem seemed to almost crackle with energy and optimism in the early 1920s. The knowledge that Harlem had, virtually overnight, become America's first great black metropolis also contributed to the sense of excitement that pervaded the community. The black jazz clubs, cabarets, and speakeasies that were sprouting up all around Harlem to meet the bustling community's demand for entertainment further contributed to the sense that an exhilarating new age was at hand. But perhaps the greatest factor in the feeling that Harlem was on the cusp of a "Negro renaissance" was the arrival on the scene of an advance guard of young, talented poets, novelists, musicians, artists, and essayists. Over the next several years, these men and women would give eloquent voice to the long-muffled dreams and frustrations of black America.

submissively to white harassment, West Indians were more likely to respond to insults and discrimination with defiance. They also expressed outrage at the severely limited economic opportunities available to non-whites in America. "On coming to the United States, the West Indian . . . is angry and amazed at the futility of seeking out certain types of employment for which he may be specially adapted," wrote Eric Walrond, an immigrant from Guyana who became a noted writer of the Harlem Renaissance. "And about the cruelest injury that could be inflicted upon him is to ask him to submit to the notion that because he is black it is useless for him to aspire to be more than a trap drummer at Small's, a Red Cap in Pennsylvania Station, or a clerk in the Bowling Green Post Office."

Disillusioned and angered by the inequities in American society, West Indian immigrants ranked among Garvey's most devoted followers. In addition, immigrants from the West Indies were key figures in the defiant response of several black communities to the race riots that broke out during the Red Summer of 1919.

Source:
Parascandola, Louis J., ed. *"Winds Can Wake Up the Dead": An Eric Walrond Reader.* Detroit, MI: Wayne State University Press, 1998.

These gifted writers and artists—Langston Hughes, Countee Cullen, Aaron Douglas, Jessie Redmon Fauset, Josephine Baker, Duke Ellington, Zora Neale Hurston, Paul Robeson, Wallace Thurman, Jean Toomer, and many others—powered the Harlem Renaissance throughout the 1920s and early 1930s. Yet they never would have made such an impact were it not for the wisdom of older black intellectuals and civil rights activists like W.E.B. Du Bois, James Weldon Johnson, Alain Locke, Arthur Schomburg, and Charles S. Johnson. "It was the brilliant insight of the men and women of the NAACP and the NUL that although the road to the ballot box, the union hall, the decent neighborhood, and the office was blocked, there were two paths that had not been barred, in part because of their very implausibility, as well as their irrelevancy to most Americans: arts and letters," wrote historian David Levering Lewis in *The Portable Harlem Renaissance Reader.*

The CRISIS

𝕿𝖊𝖓𝖙𝖍 𝕰𝖉𝖚𝖈𝖆𝖙𝖎𝖔𝖓 𝕹𝖚𝖒𝖇𝖊𝖗

JULY, 1921   FIFTEEN CENTS A COPY

The Crisis became the most influential black publication of the Harlem Renaissance era.

These men and women instinctively recognized that high-quality literature, art, and music produced by African-American writers and artists had the capacity to strengthen black pride and confidence, both of which remained under constant assault from the wider American society. Equally importantly, black leaders believed that black art and literature could be used to shatter the ethnic stereotypes that fueled white America's discriminatory attitudes toward their race. As historian Nathan Irvin Huggins observed in *Voices from the Harlem Renaissance,* they became convinced that "inequities due to race might best be removed when reasonable men saw that black men were thinkers, strivers, doers, and were cultured, like themselves."

Finally, Harlem's black leadership agreed that the civil rights cause could be greatly advanced if the bloodstream of American thought on the nation's so-called "Negro problem" received a transfusion of commentary *by blacks.* "Of all the voluminous literature on the Negro, so much is mere external view and commentary . . . that nine-tenths of it is about the Negro rather than of him, so that it is the Negro problem rather than the Negro that is known," explained Alain Locke. "Whoever wishes to see the Negro . . . in the full perspective of his achievements and possibilities, must seek the enlightenment of that self-portraiture which the present developments of Negro culture are offering."

Harlem's black leadership thus resolved to actively support black art and literature that displayed the humanity of African Americans and the bravery of their long struggle against racial oppression. This support took many forms. In recognition of the financial struggles that many of these writers and artists faced, black intellectuals helped connect them with wealthy white philanthropists who supported the civil rights cause. The patronage of these liberal whites freed many artists and writers to pursue their craft without worrying about paying the rent.

Even more importantly, Du Bois and other luminaries of the Talented Tenth used African-American magazines and newspapers to champion the prose and poetry of Hughes, Cullen, and other promising talents. The journals of the NAACP (*The Crisis,* founded in 1910) and the NUL (*Opportunity,* founded in 1922) were particularly vital to this effort. These journals provided a forum for black voices to finally be heard by large numbers of readers, and their sponsorship of literary contests brought numerous talented black writers to the attention of influential white publishers and editors.

Charles S. Johnson, who served as editor of *Opportunity* during the height of the Harlem Renaissance, summarized the impact of these magazines in his 1954 essay "The Negro Renaissance and Its Significance": "The importance of the *The Crisis* and *Opportunity Magazine* was that of providing an outlet for young Negro writers and scholars whose work was not acceptable to other established media because it could not be believed to be of standard quality despite the superior quality of much of it." Indeed, it was in the pages of these periodicals that most of the leading literary voices of the Harlem Renaissance were first heard.

Chapter Three

LITERATURE OF THE HARLEM RENAISSANCE

⬥

> Negro life is not only establishing new contacts and founding
> new centers, it is also finding a new soul. There is a fresh spir-
> itual and cultural focusing. We have, as a heralding sign, an
> unusual outburst of creative expression. There is a renewed
> race-spirit that consciously and proudly sets itself apart.
>
> —Alain Locke, *The New Negro*

Prior to the Harlem Renaissance, very few African-American writers had penetrated the consciousness of white-dominated American society. Most of the writers who did manage to garner the attention and respect of white readers were men such as Frederick Douglass and W.E.B. Du Bois, civil rights activists who used the essay form to advance their arguments for racial equality.

African-American novelists and poets, though, were practically invisible. The white publishers and literary critics who dominated the American publishing industry in the late nineteenth and early twentieth centuries doubted that white readers would read poems or novels written by blacks. In addition, many of these publishers and critics harbored their own stereotypical beliefs about the literary talents of black writers. Prior to World War I, then, only a handful of black authors, such as poet Paul Laurence Dunbar and novelist Charles W. Chesnutt, were able to slog through America's swamp of bigotry and achieve national recognition.

Dawning of a New Literary Age

By the end of World War I, however, exciting new literary rumblings could be heard in the New York City neighborhood of Harlem and other

Claude McKay was one of the first black poets to express the boiling anger that African Americans felt about their inferior status in American society.

urban centers with large black populations. Black intellectuals affiliated with the National Association for the Advancement of Colored People (NAACP), the National Urban League (NUL), and other religious and civic organizations actively supported African-American literature and art as never before. In the early 1920s, for example, the magazines of the NAACP (*Crisis*) and the NUL (*Opportunity*) were the primary artistic outlets for emerging writers such as Langston Hughes, Countee Cullen, Walter F. White, and Zora Neale Hurston, as well as better-known black writers such as Du Bois and James Weldon Johnson.

In addition, the return of black World War I veterans instilled new levels of racial pride and civil rights activity in African-American communities. One of the most famous poems of the entire Harlem Renaissance era was Claude McKay's 1919 protest work "If We Must Die," which reflected black anger over the 1919 "Red Summer" race riots. McKay's defiant poem powerfully conveyed the changing attitudes of black leaders toward the racial inequities that riddled American society.

These factors—along with the blossoming of Harlem into a thriving black "city within a city"—transformed New York City into a remarkably fertile and supportive environment for talented young African-American writers. These poets, novelists, playwrights, and essayists responded by creating works that changed American literature forever.

Early Works of the Renaissance

In 1921 Langston Hughes began his ascent to the top of the list of Renaissance literary giants with the publication of his poem "The Negro Speaks of Rivers" in *Crisis* (see Hughes biography, p. 115). Over the next several years, Hughes unveiled many of his most famous poems in the pages of *Crisis* and *Opportunity*. These eloquent, soulful works—as well as his essays and short stories—celebrated his black heritage but also condemned America's awful record of racial ignorance and hatred. Other noted Harlem Renaissance writers such as Arna Bontemps, Countee Cullen, and Gwendolyn Bennett launched their literary careers through the pages of *Crisis* and *Opportunity* during this time as well.

Another early landmark in the literature of the Harlem Renaissance was Claude McKay's 1922 poetry collection *Harlem Shadows*. This acclaimed collection, which included "If We Must Die," was one of the first works by a black writer to be published by a major national publisher (Harcourt, Brace and Company). After its publication, fellow Renaissance author (and NAACP luminary) James Weldon Johnson joined many other black intellectuals in singing McKay's praises (see Johnson biography, p. 127). "[Johnson] called upon African Americans to be proud of a poet so capable of voicing with such power the bitterness that so often rose in the heart of the race," wrote Tyrone Tillery in *Harlem Speaks*.

Johnson also advanced the cause of black literature himself by serving as editor of *The Book of American Negro Poetry* (1922). This anthology brought

James Weldon Johnson emerged as one of Harlem's most important political and literary voices in the early 1920s.

together the work of thirty-one African-American poets and included a famous essay on black literature written by Johnson himself. In this essay, Johnson clearly articulated the Talented Tenth's belief that black writers could shatter white racism's grip on American society by presenting positive images of African Americans—and by proving that blacks were capable of producing enduring artistic works.

Other black writers echoed Johnson's words. Renaissance writer George Schuyler expressed the hope that black poems, stories, and novels would forever eliminate white portrayals of blacks in which "it is only necessary to beat a tom tom or wave a rabbit's foot and he is ready to strip off his Hart, Shaffner & Marx suit, grab a spear and ride off wild-eyed on the back of a crocodile." Jessie Redmon Fauset, meanwhile, framed the advent of the Harlem Renaissance as a historic educational opportunity. "Here is an audience [white Americans] waiting to hear the truth about us," she declared. "Let us who are better qualified to present that truth than any white writer, try to do so."

Prominent writers and activists of the early Harlem Renaissance at this 1924 dinner party included (from left): Langston Hughes, Charles S. Johnson, E. Franklin Frazier, Rudolph Fisher, and Hubert T. Delaney.

Several black authors answered this call by producing notable literary works. In 1923 Jean Toomer's experimental novel *Cane* was published. This work, which skillfully moved back and forth between African-American life in the rural South and the black experience in the urban North, inspired the entire African-American writing community. One year later, Jessie Redmon Fauset published *There is Confusion*, which focused on the hopes and dreams of middle-class black Americans. Later in 1924, civil rights activist Walter F. White published *Fire in the Flint*, a powerful novel about the Jim Crow South.

"Sing, O Black Poets!"

These and other works created by black poets and novelists were received with great excitement in Harlem (see "Poetry of the Harlem Renaissance," p. 171). Religious and civil rights leaders in the community hailed their power and openly spoke about their potential for changing white attitudes about blacks. Moreover, the fast-growing body of black literature was seen as an important tool in changing black attitudes about themselves and their history. In an address to "makers of black verse," poet Frank Horne wrote in *Opportunity* in November 1924 that your task is definite, grand, and fine. You are to sing the attributes of a soul. Be superbly conscious of the many tributaries to our pulsing stream of life. You must articulate what the hidden sting of the slaver's lash leaves reverberating in its train, —the subtle hates, the burnt desires, sudden hopes, and dark despairs; you must show that the sigh is mother of the laugh they know so well. Sing, so that they might know the eyes of black babes—eyes that so sadly laugh; that they might know that we, too, like Shylock, cry when we are hurt, but with a cry distinctive, and subtly pregnant with overtones, and fraught with hidden associations. Sing, O black poets, for song is all we have!"

The Harlem Renaissance fired the imaginations of liberal white editors, publishers, and supporters of black civil rights as well. "I have a genuine faith in the future of imaginative writing among Negroes in the United States," declared Carl Van Doren in 1924. Van Doren, who served as literary editor of *The Nation* and *Century Magazine* during various phases of the Harlem Renaissance, asserted that

> this [faith] is not due to any mere personal interest in the writers of the race whom I happen to know. It is due to a feeling that the Negroes of the country are in a remarkable strategic position with reference to the new literary age which seems to be impending. Long oppressed and handicapped, they have gathered stores of emotion and are ready to burst forth with a new eloquence once they discover adequate mediums . . . The Negroes, it must be remembered, are our oldest American minority. First slavery and then neglect have forced them into a limited channel of existence. Once they find a voice, they will bring a fresh and fierce sense of reality to their vision of human life on this continent, a vision seen from a novel angle by a part of the population which cannot be duped by the bland optimism of the majority.

By the mid-1920s, the wave of literary works pouring out of Harlem and other black population centers was seeping onto the pages of some of the country's leading magazines, including *Harper's, American Mercury,* and *Century Magazine.* Small but influential literary magazines such as *Poetry* and *Palms* also promoted the works of Cullen, Hughes, Bontemps, and other talented young Harlem writers. In addition, novels and poetry anthologies written by black authors were being embraced by white-owned publishing houses such as Knopf, a New York-based firm owned by Alfred E. and Blanche Knopf.

During this same period, the editors of both *Crisis* and *Opportunity* announced complementary slates of annual literary awards that they intended to bestow on black writers and artists. These awards boosted the careers of numerous deserving writers and gave further fuel to the literary buzz swirling around the poets, novelists, essayists, and playwrights of Harlem.

Harlem—"Negro Mecca" or "Nigger Heaven"?

Perhaps the clearest evidence of the excitement surrounding the Harlem Renaissance came on March 21, 1924, when *Opportunity* editor Charles S. Johnson orchestrated a grand celebration of the new age of "Negro" writing at Manhattan's prestigious Civic Club. This historic evening brought together many of the movement's talented writers with some of America's most famous white literary figures, including H.L. Mencken, Eugene O'Neill, and Carl Van Doren.

Countee Cullen was one of many talented African American writers who published work in the groundbreaking 1925 issue of *Survey Graphic* devoted to Harlem.

One of the guests from the white literary establishment who attended the Civic Club dinner was Paul Kellogg, editor of *Survey Graphic*, a well-regarded and popular monthly magazine devoted to social issues. Kellogg was so impressed by the talent and ambition of the black attendees that he decided to devote an entire issue of his magazine to the Harlem Renaissance in particular and the state of black America in general. He invited Alain Locke, an influential African-American literary critic and scholar, to serve as guest editor of the issue (see Locke biography, p. 139).

This special edition of *Survey Graphic*, subtitled *Harlem: Mecca of the New Negro*, was published in March 1925. The issue featured a stunning range of material, including poetry contributed by Hughes, McKay, Cullen, and Angelina Grimke; a Rudolph Fisher short story about life in Harlem for recent immigrants from the South; photographs of Harlem and some of its citizens; and essays about various aspects of Harlem life from such respected voices as Walter F. White, James Weldon Johnson, Charles S. Johnson, Joel A. Rogers, and Locke (see "Alain Locke Describes the Emerging Black Culture in Harlem," p. 165). The final result, according to Carl Van Doren, was "an amazing performance. I have read it with delight and am carefully preserving it among my most valued American documents." Several months later, Locke republished the contents of the special issue—with additional material—in a popular anthology titled *The New Negro: An Interpretation.*

One year later, though, the sensation surrounding the special Harlem issue of *Survey Graphic* was eclipsed by the publication of the most controversial novel of the entire Harlem Renaissance era. The book was *Nigger Heaven,* a bestselling novel about Harlem written by white novelist Carl Van Vechten. The book triggered tremendous turmoil within Harlem's literary community and among its civil rights leadership.

Van Vechten had long been known as a friend and promoter of black writers and artists. He frequented jazz and blues clubs in Harlem before most other whites had discovered the exciting music being played there, and he invited black intellectuals and authors into his home long before the term "Harlem Renaissance" came into common usage. At some of Van Vechten's integrated parties, black friends of his such as James Weldon Johnson, Countee Cullen, and Paul Robeson sometimes even gave dramatic readings to the assembled guests.

But when *Nigger Heaven*—a term for the balcony of a segregated theater, where blacks were forced to sit—was published, many members of the Talented Tenth attacked it. Du Bois was perhaps the most vocal critic. Du Bois condemned the title of the novel as deeply insulting, and he characterized the book's contents as "an affront to the hospitality of black folk and to the intelligence of whites." He wanted novels, poems, and plays about Harlem and black America to portray African Americans as proud, industrious, and worthy of full citizenship, and he was scandalized by Van Vechten's decision to portray all aspects of Harlem—including its gritty nightclubs and criminal underworld.

Other blacks also objected to Van Vechten's book, echoing Du Bois's charge that the novel emphasized the seamier side of life in Harlem. Critic Benjamin Brawley, for example, called *Nigger Heaven* "the perfect illustration of a book that gives the facts but that does not tell the truth." But other black

Carl Van Vechten and the Renaissance

Carl Van Vechten was one of the most controversial individuals associated with the Harlem Renaissance. Born in Cedar Rapids, Iowa, on June 17, 1880, Van Vechten moved to New York City in 1906 and over the next two decades worked as a novelist and critic of music and modern dance. During this time the white writer developed a fascination with Harlem's blossoming music and literary scenes, and in the 1920s he became an important promoter of the work of some of the leading writers of the Harlem Renaissance, including Langston Hughes (with whom he developed a life-long friendship) and Wallace Thurman.

In 1926 Van Vechten's novel *Nigger Heaven* brought the author both acclaim and controversy. The book was a bestseller, and scholar Cary D. Wintz wrote in *Remembering the Harlem Renaissance* that it "almost singlehandedly created the white fascination with Harlem and African American life that characterized the 1920s." Some leading black intellectuals and civil rights leaders of the era, however, condemned the novel as a racist and destructive portrait of black life in Harlem.

In the 1930s Van Vechten became a noted portrait photographer. Many of the stars of the Harlem Renaissance posed for his camera, including Hughes, Aaron Douglas, Claude McKay, Bessie Smith, and Zora Neale Hurston, but he also took portraits of white celebrities like F. Scott Fitzgerald, Sir Laurence Olivier, and Orson Welles. A close friend to writer Gertrude Stein, Van Vechten was named her literary executor after her death in 1946. He played an important role in guiding many of her unpublished works into print in the late 1940s and 1950s. Van Vechten died in New York City in 1964.

Source:
Bernard, Emily, ed. *Remember Me to Harlem: The Letters of Langston Hughes and Carl Van Vechten, 1925-1964.* New York: Knopf, 2001.

intellectuals and authors, including Nella Larsen, Langston Hughes, Zora Neale Hurston, and James Weldon Johnson, rushed to defend Van Vechten's book as an authentic portrayal of the African-American experience in Harlem.

Even as this controversy raged, Van Vechten's book proved enormously popular with white readers. It has even been credited with being the single greatest factor in the creation of the "Negro vogue" that swept through some white urban communities in the mid-1920s. "Following the publication of [*Nigger Heaven*], white middle-class America eagerly devoured anything with a black flavor to it," wrote Cary D. Wintz in *Black Culture and the Harlem Renaissance.* "Black writers and poets suddenly found themselves pursued by publishers, exhibitions of African art brought crowds to museums and galleries, *Amos 'n' Andy* became a hit radio show, and slumming in Harlem became a favorite pastime for those looking for a sensual, exotic, and primitive thrill."

Artistic Integrity and "Advancing the Race"

The debate over the merits of *Nigger Heaven* also exposed a widening philosophical divide within Harlem's intellectual and literary communities. Many older members of the civil rights establishment—which had been so vital in promoting the careers of talented but unknown black writers—believed that African-American novelists, poets, composers, and playwrights had a moral obligation to portray blacks as smart, honest, and responsible. These black intellectuals clung to the hope that positive portrayals of black life and culture could help them in their ongoing quest to end racial segregation and discrimination in American society.

With this in mind, some influential intellectuals urged the artists and writers of the Harlem Renaissance to focus their energies on portrayals of educated, successful, and morally upright blacks. They also counseled black writers, artists, and musicians to follow European artistic and musical traditions that educated white Americans understood and appreciated. "All Art is propaganda and ever must be, despite the wailing of the purists," stated Du Bois in the December 1926 issue of the *Crisis*. "I stand in utter shamelessness and say that whatever art I have for writing has always been used for propaganda. . . . I do not care a damn for any art that is not used for propaganda."

When African-American writers violated these guidelines, they were harshly criticized by some black intellectuals. Du Bois, for example, proclaimed that he felt "nauseate[d]" and like "taking a bath" after reading Claude McKay's 1928 novel *Home to Harlem,* a work that focused on the community's ghetto dwellers. Du Bois maintained that McKay's portrayal of partying and promiscuity in Harlem's ghetto neighborhoods was a gift to white big-ots who viewed blacks as morally and intellectually inferior.

A few prominent writers of the Harlem Renaissance expressed solidarity with Du Bois. Countee Cullen wrote in *Opportunity* in 1928 that black writers who "let art portray things as they are, no matter what the consequences, no matter who is hurt" are engaging in "a blind bit of philosophy." Other writers, like Jessie Redmon Fauset, tried to set an example by keeping the focus of their works on the educated black middle-class.

Du Bois's views about the social responsibilities of black writers and artists, however, put him at odds with many other leading voices of the Harlem Renaissance. Some elder statesmen of the Talented Tenth, such as James Weldon Johnson and Alain Locke, believed that black artists should have complete artistic freedom. They assert-ed that quality art and literature—whatever its subject mat-ter—would ultimately advance the civil rights cause.

"All Art is propaganda and ever must be, despite the wailing of the purists," wrote W.E.B. Du Bois in the Crisis. "I stand in utter shamelessness and say that whatever art I have for writing has always been used for propaganda."

Many of the younger black writers at the forefront of the Harlem Renaissance also rejected Du Bois's arguments. They understood his criticisms, but the fancy dinner parties and educated conversations that took place within Harlem's finest homes were not as interesting or illuminating to them as the action that was taking place elsewhere in the commu-nity. "Harlem's black bohemia formed the essential back-drop to the black literary Renaissance," wrote Cary D. Wintz in *Black Culture and the Harlem Renaissance*. "Young black writers sub-merged themselves in the primitive black culture that flourished in the ghetto's speakeasies, ginhouses, and jazzrooms. There all of Harlem converged: the prostitute, the washwoman, the petty gangster, the poet, and the intellectual shared the blues and swayed to the beat of the jazz musicians."

Most of the movement's young writers and artists came to believe that this messy but exciting environment was more representative of black life in Harlem. In addition, they asserted that this proud and distinctive black culture should be *celebrated* rather than hidden away. Finally, these defiant young voices came to feel that conservative civil rights leaders (as well as some of their white patrons) wanted to censor or shape the content of their works in ways that threatened to destroy their artistic integrity and independence.

When Langston Hughes published "The Negro Artist and the Racial Mountain" in 1926, he ushered in a new era of literary independence for African-American writers.

The "Negro Artist's" Declaration of Independence

These yearnings for artistic independence were eloquently summarized by Langston Hughes in an essay titled "The Negro Artist and the Racial Mountain" (see "Langston Hughes Comments on Racial Identity and Artistic Integrity," p. 182). This essay, which appeared in the June 1926 issue of the *Nation*, exploded like a bombshell among the movers and shakers of the Harlem Renaissance.

At the time the essay appeared, the charismatic Hughes was already emerging as one of the literary stars of the movement. His *Weary Blues*, a collection of poetry published earlier in 1926, had featured a dazzling selection of jazz- and blues-inspired verse, and his friends and admirers included such diverse personalities as Van Vechten, Locke, and Charles S. Johnson. It was "The Negro Artist and the Racial Mountain," however, that cemented his reputation as one of the most important voices of his generation.

In this essay, Hughes flatly declared that he had no intention of letting anyone—black or white—rein in his artistic vision by telling him what subjects were suitable for black literature. He also proclaimed his love and affection for authentic black American culture, including its gritty and primitive aspects. "We younger Negro artists who create now intend to express our dark skinned selves without fear or shame," he concluded. "If white people are pleased we are glad. If they are not, it doesn't matter. We know that we are beautiful. And ugly too. The tom-tom cries and the tom-tom laughs. If colored people are pleased we are glad. If they are not their displeasure doesn't matter either."

Young black writers, poets, and artists in Harlem and around the country reveled in Hughes's words. In the months following the publication of

bratory account of Harlem's historical development into the "capital of Black America." Du Bois was also active during this time. In 1928 he published *Dark Princess,* a novel in which he restated his belief that black equality depended on the leadership of educated black elites. Walter F. White, meanwhile, contributed *Rope and Faggot* (1929), a searing study of the history of lynching in America.

Jessie Redmon Fauset continued in her role as one of the Renaissance's foremost chroniclers of black middle-class life, publishing three novels on "the better classes of Negro"—*Plum Bun* (1929), *The Chinaberry Tree* (1931), and *Comedy: American Style* (1933). Another notable female voice of the Renaissance emerged during this time as well. Nella Larsen's two novels, *Quicksand* (1928) and *Passing* (1929), explored the struggles of mixed-race people to navigate between America's black and white worlds (see Larsen biography, p. 134). Nearly a century later, these thoughtful, gracefully written works are widely regarded as two of the best novels of the entire Renaissance era.

The novels of Jessie Redmon Fauset focused on the trials and triumphs of middle-class African Americans.

Another acclaimed novel of the late 1920s was Rudolph Fisher's *The Walls of Jericho* (1928). Previously known primarily as a short story writer and composer of music, Fisher showcased his talent for showing the humanity of all of Harlem's black residents, rich and poor, in his first novel. He followed up this acclaimed work with 1932's *Conjure-Man Dies,* which is widely regarded as the first African-American detective novel.

The same year that *Conjure-Man Dies* appeared, Sterling Brown, who spent much of the Renaissance era in Washington, D.C., published *Southern*

Road. This acclaimed book of poetry used Southern black dialect to celebrate black folk culture. Another writer who became known during this period for her usage of black dialect and her fascination with Southern roots was Hurston. Prolific and controversial, Hurston released several important works during the final years of the Renaissance, including the novel *Jonah's Gourd Vine* (1934), a collection of black folk songs and folklore called *Mules and Men* (1935), and the novel *Their Eyes Were Watching God* (1937).

Cullen published a wide range of works during this period as well, from his usual lyrical poetry (as seen in 1929's *The Black Christ, and Other Poems)* to the 1932 novel *One Way to Heaven.* But the work of Claude McKay, which reveled in the blood and sweat of working-class Harlem, was far more popular with readers. His 1928 novel *Home to Harlem,* which he wrote while living in France, was the first U.S. bestseller written by a black author. *Home to Harlem* was memorable not only for its focus on Harlem's struggling underclass, but also for its bitter attacks on the upper-class black intellectuals who had made the Renaissance possible in the first place.

Wallace Thurman published two novels during the waning years of the movement. His 1929 novel *The Blacker the Berry* tackled the explosive subject of color discrimination within the urban black community, but it also reflected the author's conviction that common folks and their experiences were the spiritual foundation of black America. Three years later, Thurman published *Infants of the Spring,* a scathing satire of the Harlem Renaissance and its leadership. In addition, *Harlem,* a play written by Thurman and William Jourdan Rapp about the big-city struggles of a black family from the South, opened at the Apollo Theater on Broadway in 1929 and became an instant hit.

Finally, Langston Hughes, the poet laureate of the Harlem Renaissance, remained prolific and productive throughout the late 1920s and early 1930s. His works during this time included novels (the autobiographical *Not Without Laughter,* 1930), poetry (1932's *The Dream Keeper and Other Poems*), and plays (*Mulatto,* which debuted on Broadway in 1935). In virtually all of these works, Hughes continued to combine poetry and prose with the sound and spirit of black music in dynamic and exciting ways. "[Hughes] sought to fuse the vitality of popular black culture with the energy of political commitment at the sides of the black masses," explained Monica Michlin in *Temples for Tomorrow.* Hughes was also one of the few writers in the movement to make significant contributions to black literature after the mid-1930s, when the literary component of the Harlem Renaissance drew to a quiet close.

The writing associated with the Harlem Renaissance dried up and faded away for several reasons. The economic struggles of the Great Depression made it much more difficult for black writers to support themselves. The deaths of talented individuals like Rudolph Fisher, Wallace Thurman, and James Weldon Johnson also hurt the movement, as did the longstanding and bitter internal debate over artistic integrity and representations of black life. Finally, Jean Toomer, Nella Larsen, and many other writers associated with the Harlem Renaissance simply drifted away over time, to new cities or new careers or new thematic interests in their writing.

Ultimately, the spirit that drove the literary Renaissance that took place in Harlem during the 1920s and early 1930s simply could not survive these departures. The key to the movement's success—despite its history of internal quarrels and differences—had always been the *collective* strength of its poets, novelists, playwrights, and essayists, rather than that of a single individual or institution.

Chapter Four

MUSIC AND ART OF THE HARLEM RENAISSANCE

—◦◦◦◦◦◦—

The Negro is bringing about an entirely new national concep-
tion of himself; he has placed himself in an entirely new light
before the American people. I do not think it too much to say
that through artistic achievement the Negro has found a means
of getting at the very core of the prejudice against him . . .

—James Weldon Johnson,
"Racial Prejudice and the Negro Artist"

At the same time that black political activists were lobbying for social
change and black writers were documenting the hopes, dreams, and frustrations of African Americans from all walks of life, black artists, musicians,
dancers, and composers were putting their own stamp on the Harlem Renaissance. It was during this period that black painters and sculptors achieved
critical and popular success in the United States for the first time. Moreover,
blues and jazz—musical genres that owed their very existence to African-
American musicians and singers—burst into prominence during this time. "It
is impossible to imagine the Harlem Renaissance without its music," wrote
scholar Cary Wintz in *Harlem Speaks*. "Jazz and the blues provided the background music for almost every event in the Harlem Renaissance. . . . Poets
and writers depicted jazz joints, musicians, and blues singers in their writing,
while artists painted them. Music was everywhere."

The Blossoming of Jazz and Blues

Blues, ragtime, and jazz are all forms of African-American folk music
that trace their roots to the system of slavery that dominated the American

Louis Armstrong was one of many talented African-American blues and jazz artists who descended on New York City during the Renaissance era.

South prior to the Civil War. Blues songs developed from the sorrow-filled laments that were sung by slaves on plantations all across the South. "Ragtime"—music played in syncopated or ragged time—evolved from the call-and-response patterns of slave work songs. Jazz music, meanwhile, took elements of both blues and ragtime and joined them with traditional black spirituals and an emphasis on musical improvisation.

Important early black composers such as W.C. Handy, known as the "father of the blues," and ragtime giant Scott Joplin spent most of their careers far from New York City. Joplin wrote "Maple Leaf Rag" and other famous ragtime songs in St. Louis, Missouri, while Handy was based for much of his career in Memphis, Tennessee. But the musical forms developed by Handy, Joplin, and other early blues and jazz pioneers in Memphis, Chicago, Kansas City, New Orleans, and other cities eventually made their way to New York City in general and Harlem in particular.

The sounds of these musical innovations first wafted out of New York clubs in the first two decades of the twentieth century. Bandleaders and composers like Jelly Roll Morton, Duke Ellington, Louis Armstrong, James Reese Europe, and Fletcher Henderson descended on the city from all points of the country, attracted by the vibrant nightclub scene and Harlem's growing reputation as the "capital of black America" (see Ellington biography, p. 110). By the early 1920s, white and black audiences alike were flocking to clubs and concert halls like never before to revel in these distinctively African-American musical forms.

The "Jazz Age" reached its zenith in the United States in the 1920s due to a wide range of factors. The talented musicians and composers that gathered in Harlem and other cities drew energy and inspiration from one another, sparking the creation of a mighty stream of exciting new music. Growing white fascination with "Negro" culture also contributed to the popularity of jazz and blues, as did the poetry and stories of Langston Hughes and other black writers. In many of their literary works, jazz and blues music was presented as the heartbeat of the "New Negroes"—confident and self-aware African Americans who were determined to assert both their civil rights and their pride in their ethnic heritage.

The arrival of Prohibition in 1920 also played a role in the meteoric rise of black musicians like Duke Ellington and Louis Armstrong, and black singers such as Ethel Waters, Gladys Bentley, and Bessie Smith (see Smith biography, p. 150). The exuberant, emotional rhythms of blues and jazz struck a chord with black and white Americans who had emerged from the misery, hardship, and death of World War I with a renewed enthusiasm for drinking, dancing, and other simple pleasures of life. The federal government's decision to ban the sale and consumption of alcoholic beverages thus spawned a tremendous proliferation of clubs and "speakeasies"—illegal taverns—in New York City and other American cities where patrons could consume alcohol in defiance of U.S. law. Jazz and blues music seemed a perfect complement to the rebellious spirit that saturated these establishments

Bandleaders and composers like Jelly Roll Morton, Duke Ellington, Louis Armstrong, James Reese Europe, and Fletcher Henderson descended on the city from all points of the country, attracted by the vibrant nightclub scene and Harlem's growing reputation as the "capital of black America."

Finally, technological innovation and industrialization were key factors in the rise of jazz and blues. For many Americans, the bouncy rhythms and improvised melodies of jazz music seemed to embody the country's quickening economic pulse and growing industrial power. In addition, jazz came along at a time when the communications and entertainment industries were being revolutionized by technological advances. Phonograph records and commercial radio, for example, enabled jazz orchestras and blues singers based in New York, Chicago, and New Orleans to spread their music to American towns and cities thousands of miles away.

Shuffle Along

The first and perhaps greatest musical event of the entire Harlem Renaissance era was *Shuffle Along*, a jazz musical written, composed, and performed

Ragtime composers Eubie Blake (left) and Noble Sissle wrote the music and lyrics to *Shuffle Along,* the popular Broadway play often credited with opening white America's eyes to the talent of African-American entertainers.

by African Americans. This Broadway smash hit, which opened in 1921 and enjoyed a run of 504 electrifying performances, served notice that a new age of American music was dawning. It also "legitimized the African-American musical, proving to producers and managers that audiences would pay to see African-American talent on Broadway," wrote Jo Tanner for the online site *Drop Me Off in Harlem.*

Back in nineteenth-century America, the only theatrical avenues open to black actors and performers had been vaudeville and burlesque stages and minstrel shows. On these stages, black entertainers (and white entertainers who blackened their faces in crude imitation of blacks) offered up the most stereotypical portraits of African Americans. Almost without exception, blacks were portrayed as ignorant, childlike, and eager to please their white superiors.

This state of affairs began to change just before the turn of the century, when *A Trip to Coontown* opened in 1898 in New York City. This theatrical production, written by a black composer named Robert A. Cole, was the first musical production in U.S. history to be primarily organized, written, produced, and managed by blacks. Cole also helped launch two other black theatrical productions that appeared on New York stages over the next decade— *The Shoo-fly Regiment* (1906) and *The Red Moon* (1908).

Other important early figures in the black theater in New York included composer Will Marion Cook and lyricist Paul Laurence Dunbar, who collaborated on *Clorindy—The Origin of the Cakewalk* (1898); and Bert Williams and George Nash Walker, who produced such shows as *In Dahomey* (1902) and *Bandanna Land* (1908). In the 1910s, though, not a single theatrical production written, composed, or produced by African Americans appeared on Broadway.

In many respects, then, *Shuffle Along* seemed to come out of nowhere when it took Broadway by storm in 1921. This revue, written by Flournoy Miller and Aubrey Lyles, with music and lyrics by the ragtime vaudeville team of Noble Sissle and Eubie Blake, featured a crowd-pleasing blend of lively jazz dancing, spirited singing, and romantic drama. It dazzled black and white patrons alike and launched the careers of Florence Mills and Josephine Baker.

The joyful spirit and stunning showmanship that swirled across the stage during each performance of *Shuffle Along* also influenced Countee Cullen, Langston Hughes, and other talented young writers of the Harlem Renaissance. "*Shuffle Along* . . . became a smash on Broadway at about the same time Cullen and Hughes were making their initial bows," recalled fellow writer Arna Bontemps in *The Awakening: A Memoir*. "A happier conjunction could scarcely have been imagined, and the impact of this production, the wide popularity of its songs, the dazzling talent of its performers almost lifted the boy poets off their feet. . . . *Shuffle Along* was an announcement, an overture to an era of hope."

New Opportunities in American Theater

Shuffle Along was so successful that Broadway promoters rushed to find other African-American musicals for their stages. In 1923 Miller and Lyles starred

After first attracting attention for her performance in *Shuffle Along,* African-American singer/dancer Josephine Baker became an international star.

in *Runnin' Wild,* which became most famous for launching the Charleston dance craze across the nation. One year later, Josephine Baker vaulted to stardom in Sissle and Blake's *Chocolate Dandies.* This role enabled Baker to relocate to the racially progressive nation of France, where her fabulous singing and sexy stage persona made her an international star. Seven other African-American musicals also premiered at various Broadway venues between the debut of *Shuffle Along* and the end of 1924. For the remainder of the decade, musical revues written, directed, and performed by African American artists regularly appeared on Broadway.

The success of these musical revues led to the opening of several jazz dancing schools in Harlem and other parts of New York. White customers flocked to these schools to learn the Charleston, the Black Bottom, the Lindy Hop, and other dances popularized by black performers. Affluent whites also began to drift up to Harlem, where club after club was opening to take advantage of the sudden craze for jazz and blues music (and the thirst for illegal alcohol).

White visitors to Harlem could find Bessie Smith, Ma Rainey, and Gladys Bentley belting out blues songs in small speakeasies, and legendary jazz players such as saxophonist Coleman Hawkins and trumpeter Louis Armstrong practicing their art in smoky cabarets. These same dance halls and clubs attracted large numbers of African-American patrons as well. "Among blacks, far more people knew who Ma Rainey was than James Weldon Johnson or even Langston Hughes," explained historian Cary D. Wintz in *Black Culture and the Harlem Renaissance.* "Singers and the top musicians became celebrities."

Black actors and actresses also enjoyed greater success than ever before in the 1920s. In 1920 black actor Charles Gilpin played the starring role in *The*

Emperor Jones, a play by famed playwright Eugene O'Neill. Four years later, Paul Robeson accepted O'Neill's offer of the lead in *All God's Chillun Got Wings*, a bold, challenging drama about interracial marriage. This role, combined with his performance in a 1924 revival of *The Emperor Jones*, established Robeson as a theatrical star. Over the next three decades, Robeson's skills as an actor, his magnificent singing voice, and his gradual turn to Communist-based political activism made him one of the country's biggest—and most controversial—celebrities (see Robeson biography, p. 143).

Other milestones in serious black theater during the 1920s included the 1923 Broadway debut of *The Chip Woman's Fortune*, a drama by black playwright Willis Richardson that was performed by the National Ethiopian Art Players; the 1925 drama *Appearances* by Garland Anderson; Paul Green's Pulitzer Prize-winning drama *In Abraham's Bosom*, which debuted in 1927

Paul Robeson, seen here in a London production of *Othello*, was one of the greatest stars of the stage in the 1920s and 1930s.

with an all-black cast including Jules Bledsoe and Rose McClendon; and the 1929 Broadway hit *Harlem*, which was co-written by the fiery black writer Wallace Thurman and white playwright William Jourdan Rapp. In addition, important black acting troupes and organizations such as the Negro Experimental Theatre, the Negro Art Theatre, and the National Colored Players all were founded in the 1920s.

Black Music and Black Intellectuals

The runaway success of *Shuffle Along* and other African-American musicals, combined with the rising popularity of Harlem-based singers, musicians, and orchestras, attracted the notice of New York City's leading black intellectuals. These men and women—W.E.B. Du Bois, Jessie Redmon Fauset, Alain Locke, Charles Johnson, James Weldon Johnson, and others—believed that a historic opportunity to reshape white attitudes about blacks was at hand. They asserted that the emergence of talented black singers, musicians, and composers could help lift the social fortunes of *all* African Americans by increasing white respect for the artistic capacities of blacks. They had made these same arguments about black literature over the previous few years, so it was not a stretch for them to expand the list of race-empowering artistic pursuits to include music.

But many black intellectuals were uncomfortable with the jazz and blues music pouring out of Harlem's clubs. They worried that these musical forms were too unrefined and primitive. Some activists even asserted that jazz music damaged the image of African Americans. These individuals wanted to highlight other musical and theatrical accomplishments by black musicians and composers instead. They sought to emphasize events such as the debut of James P. Johnson's *Yamekraw: A Negro Rhapsody* at Carnegie Hall in 1929 and the careers of black symphonic composers such as Florence Price, Margaret Bonds, and William Grant Still. When Alain Locke's influential 1925 anthology *The New Negro* was published, the book barely even acknowledged the existence of jazz and blues giants such as Bessie Smith and Duke Ellington.

Other leading black voices of the Harlem Renaissance embraced jazz and blues music, though. They felt that this music had a uniquely African-American character, and that the rhythms of blues and jazz reflected both the sorrowful history and proud spirit of black Americans. Writing in *The Big Sea,* author Langston Hughes recalled that he desperately wanted the "blare of Negro jazz bands [to] penetrate the closed ears of colored intellectuals." By the late 1920s, Hughes and other leading writers of the Renaissance were frequently incorporating jazz music rhythms and cabaret settings into their poems, short stories, and novels. And as scholars Michel Feith and Geneviève Fabre point out in *Temples for Tomorrow,* even intellectuals who worried that blues and jazz would be "seen as the primitive expression of an uncivilized people" admitted that the music was a "distinctive Negro art form" and "the symbol of a freedom from restraint that many longed to achieve."

Famous Clubs of Harlem

At the peak of the Harlem Renaissance in the late 1920s, many Harlem nightspots became famous throughout New York City. One street on the south-

A'Lelia Walker and The Dark Tower

During the peak of the Harlem Renaissance, no hostess was as popular or notorious as A'Lelia Walker. Born on June 6, 1885, in Vicksburg, Mississippi, Walker was the only child of Madam C.J. Walker, one of America's first wealthy black entrepreneurs. Walker's line of hair-care products for black women made her a wealthy woman. When she died in 1919, A'Lelia inherited her mother's fortune, which included a Harlem townhouse and a country mansion outside New York City.

During the 1920s the flamboyant heiress became known as Harlem's greatest party-giver. She threw elegant and lavish parties at her country mansion, but the gatherings at her Harlem townhouse were even more spectacular in some ways. Walker redecorated much of the townhouse into a vast salon of music, poetry, drinking, and dancing that she called the Dark Tower, in honor of the title of a regular column that Countee Cullen wrote for *Opportunity* magazine. Some names on Walker's guest lists for parties scandalized the more conservative members of the Harlem elite, but the six-foot-tall hostess seemed to enjoy their disapproval. Every party at the Dark Tower was packed with poets and gangsters, whites and blacks, and straight and homosexual guests, and Walker savored every glamorous moment. "A'Lelia Walker was the joy-goddess of Harlem's 1920's," recalled Langston Hughes in *The Big Sea*.

Walker's parties at the Dark Tower ended with the onset of the Great Depression. She moved out of the townhouse in 1930, and on August 16, 1931, she died unexpectedly in Long Branch, New Jersey, while visiting friends.

ern end of Harlem, 133rd Street between Lenox Avenue and 7th Avenue, housed a particularly dense concentration of cabarets and clubs. Notable nightclubs on this street, popularly known as Jungle Alley, Paradise Valley, or simply The Street, included Barron's, the Catagonia Club, and the Clam House.

Other well-known nightclubs were sprinkled all around Harlem. The Lenox Club, the Stork Club, Smalls' Paradise, the Bamboo Inn, and the Renaissance Casino and Ballroom all attracted large numbers of patrons during the heyday of the Harlem Renaissance. The two biggest names in Harlem nightclubs, however, were the Cotton Club and the Savoy Ballroom. These two clubs, which were almost polar opposites from one another in their approach to issues of race, became famous across the United States—and even as far away as Europe.

The Cotton Club opened in September 1923 on the northeast corner of Lenox Avenue and 142nd Street, and it instantly became one of the most glamorous—and notorious—establishments in all of New York City. Owned by Prohibition-era gangster Owen Madden, the Cotton Club was decorated in spectacular fashion to attract wealthy downtowners. It also boasted appearances from some of the era's greatest black entertainers. From the early 1920s through the late 1930s, the house orchestra was led by such musical giants as Fletcher Henderson, Duke Ellington, and Cab Calloway.

Madden, however, established a whites-only policy regarding paying customers. The only black people who were permitted to enter the club—which was located in the heart of "black America"—were cooks, waiters, busboys, and entertainers. The club's management also restricted membership in its female chorus line to light-skinned African-American women who were presumably more attractive to the white clientele. These employment restrictions, combined with the "Southern plantation" decorative scheme, produced an atmosphere that reeked of racism. Calloway, whose orchestra replaced Ellington's in the early 1930s, recalled in his autobiography *Of Minnie the Moocher & Me* that

> the bandstand was a replica of a southern mansion, with large white columns and a backdrop painted with weeping willows and slave quarters. The band played on the veranda of the mansion, and in front of the veranda, down a few steps, was the dance floor, which was also used for the shows. The waiters were dressed in red tuxedos, like butlers in a southern mansion, and the tables were covered with red-and-white-checked gingham tablecloths. There were huge cut-crystal chandeliers, and the whole set was like the sleepy-time-down-South during slavery. Even the name, Cotton Club, was supposed to convey the southern feeling. I suppose the idea was to make whites who came to the club feel like they were being catered to and entertained by black slaves.

The Savoy Ballroom was one of the jewels of the Harlem nightclub scene during the Renaissance era.

The existence of the segregationist Cotton Club within America's most famous black neighborhood angered and frustrated many Harlem residents. The cabaret survived for only a few short years, though. One year after the Harlem riots of 1935, the Cotton Club moved to a new downtown location. Few Harlem residents were sorry to see it go. Four years later, it closed its doors forever.

The Savoy Ballroom, meanwhile, was treasured by the people of Harlem. Occupying an entire city block, the Savoy opened on Lenox Avenue in March 1926. The Savoy's huge dance floor, elegant furnishings, and parade of top talent made it a premier destination for partygoers. Another important element in the Savoy's tremendous popularity was the owners' decision to open their doors to people of all colors and classes. This policy, which created a festive atmosphere in which white and black patrons danced side by side, made the Savoy a delightful oasis of integration in 1920s America (see "Frankie Manning Remembers the Savoy Ballroom," p. 188).

Visitors to the Savoy's plush ballroom were treated to performances from many of the leading entertainers of the Jazz Age, including bands led by Fletcher Henderson, Louis Armstrong, Chick Webb, Benny Goodman, Duke Ellington, Tommy Dorsey, and Count Basie. Famous singers who performed at the Savoy during the Renaissance era included Bessie Smith, Ella Fitzgerald, and Billie Holiday. The ballroom finally closed in 1958, thirty-two years after its debut.

Black Painters and Sculptors

As in the worlds of music and literature, black art became much more vital and visible during the Harlem Renaissance. But unlike the era's black music and literature, which first blossomed in the 1910s and early 1920s, the first sustained wave of important African-American art did not emerge until the late 1920s. Prior to the early 1920s, few African Americans worked as sculptors or painters. Those individuals who did work in these media rarely tackled racial themes or tried to create art that reflected their African past. Works such as Meta Warrick Fuller's 1914 sculpture *Ethiopia Awakening,* which depicted a proud black woman adorned with the headdress of an Egyptian queen, were rarities.

In the mid-1920s, though, the first stirrings of a uniquely African-American vision in sculpture and painting could be seen. This growing interest in African artistic traditions—and their relation to modern black America—was fueled in large part by Alain Locke, one of the primary architects of the Harlem Renaissance. "Locke encouraged [black] artists to include the emotion and drama of African art, to make the work passionate, to move those who experienced it," wrote Amy H. Kirschke in *Temples for Tomorrow.* "He believed African art was a tangible way to teach African-Americans, indeed all Americans, about the connection of black America to Africa and Africa's rich culture."

Black literary magazines were an important early outlet for this new direction in black art. *Opportunity,* which was produced by the National Urban League (NUL), and *Crisis,* the literary magazine of the National Association for the Advancement of Colored People (NAACP), provided black painters and illustrators with a valuable avenue by which they could show their work to the public. This exposure, combined with modest growth in illustrating opportunities in support of black novels, poetry collections, and theatrical productions, launched the careers of major Renaissance-era artists like Aaron Douglas.

Ironically, one of the most influential early collections of illustrations to explore African themes was created by Winold Reiss, a German-born artist. The African-based motifs of the illustrations he provided for Alain Locke's special March 1925 Harlem issue of *Survey Graphic* greatly influenced Douglas, who is today widely regarded as the greatest of the Harlem Renaissance artists (see Douglas biography, p. 97). During the late 1920s and 1930s, Douglas's illustrations and paintings—which relied heavily on hard geometric edges, African cultural themes, and the spirit of African-American jazz

The art of Aaron Douglas, seen here on the cover of a Claude Mckay novel, became closely associated with the Harlem Renaissance.

music—became closely identified with the Renaissance. His paintings and illustrations appeared everywhere, from the pages of James Weldon Johnson's monumental book of poetic sermons, *God's Trombones,* to the 135th Street branch of the New York Public Library, where he created his famous four-panel mural *Aspects of Negro Life* in 1934.

Institutions such as the Harmon Foundation (founded by white businessman William E. Harmon in 1922) also provided valuable support. The Harmon Foundation bestowed annual cash prizes to African Americans in the visual arts, business and industry, literature, science, and other areas. In 1928 it also sponsored the first-ever American art exhibition composed entirely of works by black artists. Douglas, sculptor Augusta Savage, painter Palmer C. Hayden, and many other prominent black artists of the Harlem Renaissance directly benefited from the assistance of the Harmon Foundation. Another important group was the Harlem Artists Guild, an organization of black painters and sculptors founded in 1935.

Douglas remains the most famous artist associated with the Renaissance. But many other artists made important contributions. In addition to Savage and Hayden, painters and graphic designers affiliated with the movement included Archibald J. Motley, Hale Woodruff, Laura Wheeler Waring, William H. Johnson, Jacob Lawrence, and Lois Mailou Jones. In the area of sculpture, important black artists of the period included Elizabeth Prophet, Selma Burke, Sargent Claude Johnson, and Richmond Barthe.

Black Artists in the City of Light

Prior to the Great Depression, African-American visual artists were scattered all across the United States and Europe. France remained a particularly welcoming place for African-American artists. Savage, Douglas, Woodruff, Hayden, Motley, Johnson, and many other black painters and sculptors spent extended periods of time working and studying in Paris. The godfather of this expatriate community was painter Henry Ossawa Tanner, who had lived in Paris since the 1890s. In the so-called "City of Light," Tanner and these other artists basked in a racially tolerant culture that prized intellectual and artistic achievement.

The economic difficulties of the Depression, however, forced many of these artists to return to the United States. It was at this time that New York City became a true center of African-American artistic activity and education. Important new galleries and schools for black sculptors, painters, and visual artists opened during this period. In addition, grants from the Works Progress Administration (WPA), a New Deal program designed to help lift America out of the economic wreckage of the Depression, were instrumental in nurturing artists like Lawrence and Romare Bearden in the late 1930s.

Today, the record of visual art from the Harlem Renaissance era is not viewed as being as influential as the African-American literature and music that came out of that same period. Still, many significant paintings, sculptures, and other artistic works were created during this time. Scholars note that much of this art is imbued with a remarkable sense of optimism and racial pride. Indeed, many black artists of the era pursued their craft in a spirit similar to one articulated by Aaron Douglas in a letter to poet Langston Hughes, one of his closest friends:

> Let's bare our arms and plunge them deep through laughter,
> through pain, through sorrow, through hope, through disap-

Harlem's Photographer

Born in Lenox, Massachusetts, on June 29, 1886, James Van Der Zee grew up to become the foremost photographer of Harlem and its residents during the Harlem Renaissance era. A fine pianist and violinist, Van Der Zee first moved to Harlem in 1906 to pursue a career in music. Financial struggles led him to take a job as a darkroom technician at a department store in Newark, New Jersey. The job rekindled a childhood interest in photography, and in 1917 he opened his own photography studio on 135th Street in the heart of Harlem.

For the next two decades, Van Der Zee used his camera to document all aspects of Harlem's social, economic, and cultural life, from high-society parties and weddings to street scenes. Many of the leading writers, activists, musicians, and civic leaders of the Harlem Renaissance posed for him during these years.

Van Der Zee was particularly skilled at capturing the confidence and pride of Harlem residents who loved living in America's most famous black neighborhood. He composed his portraits carefully, and many of his works showed a master's touch for hand-tinting and retouching photographs in ways that put his subjects in their best light. Van Der Zee's body of work celebrated Harlem and its people by portraying the community as successful, happy, and dignified.

Van Der Zee's fortunes declined in the 1950s, and by the late 1960s he was retired and leading an impoverished existence. But a 1969 Metropolitan Museum of Art exhibition called *Harlem on My Mind* brought renewed attention to his early work. He resumed his photography career in the 1970s and received several prestigious awards during that decade. He died in Washington, D.C., on May 15, 1983.

pointment, into the very depths of the souls of our people and drag forth material crude, rough, neglected. Then let's sing it, dance it, write it, paint it. Let's do the impossible. Let's create something transcendentally material, mystically objective. Earthy. Spiritually earthy. Dynamic.

Chapter Five

THE END OF THE HARLEM RENAISSANCE

I have been seeing a few of the younger writers and artists [around New York City], notably Gwennie Bennett who was in the thick of the Harlem Renaissance and we all of us feel more or less at loose ends.

—Claude Mckay

There was no specific event or date that brought the Harlem Renaissance to a close. The Renaissance had always been an abstract concept, even though it was rooted in the real efforts and accomplishments of numerous activists, writers, artists, musicians, ministers, and entrepreneurs in the neighborhood of Harlem, the city of New York, and around the world. Since "the movement itself was . . . based on personal commitments and loyalties rather than on a single identifiable person or institution, it is difficult to pinpoint the moment of its death," explained Cary D. Wintz in *Black Culture and the Harlem Renaissance.*

This basic reality explains why scholars of the Harlem Renaissance have differed so dramatically in judging the life span of the movement. Some insist that for all practical purposes, the Renaissance ended with the onset of the Great Depression in 1929. These historians claim that the economic turmoil of that era silenced many of Harlem's leading voices. Others assert that the Harlem Riot of 1935 brought the Renaissance to a grim and despairing end. Other scholars, though, point out that Zora Neale Hurston, Langston Hughes, Aaron Douglas, Jacob Lawrence, and numerous singers and musicians who were associated with the Harlem Renaissance enjoyed thriving careers well into the late 1930s and early 1940s (and in some cases, far beyond that).

Historians note, however, that even the leading figures in the Harlem Renaissance agree that the movement lost much of its vitality during the course of the 1930s. And these luminaries cite many of the same reasons for its decline: crushing poverty in Harlem itself, the death of several leading figures in the movement, and unquenchable artistic yearning to explore new issues and thematic boundaries.

A Community in Turmoil

Many black New Yorkers were justifiably proud of Harlem in the 1930s. The community's music and nightlife had attracted the admiration of whites from around the world, and its leading writers and activists had proved that racist beliefs in white intellectual and moral superiority over African Americans were fraudulent. James Weldon Johnson's 1930 book *Black Manhattan,* which traced the history of Harlem's emergence as the nation's center of black culture, reflected this pride and sense of accomplishment in every chapter.

Successful entertainers and entrepreneurs in Harlem also spoke of the community with great pride. "Harlem in the 1930s was the hottest place in the country," recalled bandleader Cab Calloway in *Of Minnie the Moocher & Me.*

> All the music and dancing you could want. And all the high-life people were there. It was *the* place for a Negro to be. God knows it wasn't such a ball for everyone. There were a hell of a lot of poor Negroes, too. But still, no matter how poor, you could walk down Seventh Avenue or across 125th Street on a Sunday afternoon after church and check out the women in their fine clothes and the young dudes all decked out in their spats and gloves and tweeds and Homburgs. People knew how to dress, the streets were clean and tree-lined, and there were so few cars that they were no problem. . . . Harlem was like that—a warm, clean, lovely place where thousands of black folks, poor and rich, lived together and enjoyed the life.

Underneath the glitter of the nightclubs and the pride that black people felt in having a neighborhood that was truly their own, however, Harlem suffered from serious social and economic problems in the 1920s and 1930s.

One factor in Harlem's difficulties was overpopulation. The community's reputation made it a favorite destination for Southern blacks looking to make a new start, but demand for housing became so great that landlords were able to charge inflated rental rates for apartments. Many Harlemites responded by subdividing apartments, which made for even greater congestion. The overcrowding—and related sanitary problems—triggered serious downturns in community health. By the early 1930s the average infant mortality rate for blacks in New York City was more than twice as high as it was for whites. The death rate of the city's black residents from tuberculosis was far higher than it was in large southern cities like Atlanta and Houston—and nearly five times higher than that of white New York City residents. The syphilis rate in Harlem was nine times higher than it was in white Manhattan, and black New Yorkers were twice as likely as whites to be stricken with typhoid fever or pneumonia. These various health issues were made worse by the fact that the sole public health facility in the 200,000-member community, Harlem General Hospital, had only 273 beds.

Residents of Harlem, such as these three members of a neighborhood social club, took great pride in their community.

Harlem's reputation as a center of economic vitality for blacks also proved to be a mirage. Most of the business establishments in Harlem were actually owned by whites who lived outside the community. Those businesses that were owned by African Americans were usually modest, both in terms of revenue and the number of workers they employed. This failure to build a business environment that would attract large numbers of middle-class blacks came back to haunt Harlem during the economic straits of the Depression.

Many white-owned businesses in Harlem, meanwhile, only hired blacks as porters, maids, elevator operators, or other menial positions. They exclud-

Harlem boasted many businesses in the 1920s and 1930s, but few of them were actually owned by African Americans.

ed African Americans from managerial roles and other positions that promised higher wages. And the fierce competition for jobs in Harlem enabled these same business establishments to impose low wages and fire anyone who dared to complain about poor working conditions. Some corporations that profited enormously from black Harlemites refused to hire any African Americans at all. Scholar Cary D. Wintz pointed out in *Black Culture and the Harlem Renaissance* that in 1935 the Metropolitan Life Insurance Company did not employ a single black man or woman—even though it insured more than 100,000 blacks in Harlem alone.

The economic vulnerability of Harlem's black residents was hidden somewhat during the late 1920s, when prosperous white downtowners spent huge sums of money in the neighborhood's cabarets and restaurants. The Great Depression that began in 1929, though, led many whites to curtail their visits to the cabarets. Book purchases and other economic activities that sustained struggling Harlem Renaissance writers also dropped off significantly during this time. "The depression brought everybody down a peg or two," summarized Langston Hughes in *The Big Sea*. "And the Negro had but few pegs to fall."

The end of Prohibition in 1933 further accelerated Harlem's downward economic spiral. When alcohol sales and consumption became legal again, whites stopped traveling to Harlem to indulge their taste for alcohol, and dozens of speakeasies and cabarets around Harlem shuttered their doors. Black musicians and singers who had not already abandoned Harlem for more lucrative downtown gigs were forced to move on to other venues and cities at this time.

The community would have been better equipped to absorb these blows if its residents were educated. But white politicians had zoned New York's schools to keep the races segregated, and black students did not receive the resources or opportunities provided to white students. These educational inequities further contributed to Harlem's slide, and by the mid-1930s Harlem was suffering from high rates of crime, drug addiction, and juvenile delinquency.

A Fragile Environment

Harlem's self-image suffered in other ways as well during the late 1920s and early 1930s. The influx of whites into its nightclubs and restaurants transformed Harlem into a glamorous destination and provided welcome injections of money into the community. But the opening of the whites-only Cotton Club and the flood of whites into other cabarets and clubs damaged Harlem's treasured self-image as an independent black refuge that could go about its business without worrying about whites living in the "outside" world.

In August 1927 Harlem Renaissance writer Rudolph Fisher examined this phenomenon in an article for *American Mercury*. In Fisher's piece, titled "The Caucasian Storms Harlem," he wrote that

> time and again, since I've returned to live in Harlem, I've been one of a party of four Negroes who went to this or that Harlem cabaret, and on each occasion we've been the only Negro guests in the place. The managers don't hesitate to say that it is

upon these predominant white patrons that they depend for success. These places therefore are no longer mine but theirs. Not that I'm barred, any more than they were seven or eight years ago. Once known, I'm even welcome, just as some of them used to be. But the complexion of the place is theirs, not mine. I? Why, I am actually stared at, I frequently feel uncomfortable and out of place, and when I go out on the floor to dance I am lost in a sea of white faces.

The literary, artistic, and political movements associated with the Harlem Renaissance also showed widening cracks during this period. From the outset, the Renaissance had been a diffuse movement with no clearly defined goals or leadership. In fact, some individuals closely associated with the Harlem Renaissance were only vaguely familiar with the views and works of other individuals who were reputed to be leading voices of the movement. As musician Cab Calloway admitted in his autobiography, "those of us in the music and entertainment business were vaguely aware that something exciting was happening [in black literature], but we weren't directly involved. I mean we had all heard about Langston Hughes and read his poetry, but his was a very different kind of world. . . . We were working hard on our thing and they were working hard on theirs."

Silenced Voices and Different Priorities

The Harlem Renaissance movement also suffered from the loss of some of its leading voices during the 1930s. Wallace Thurman, Rudolph Fisher, and James Weldon Johnson all died before the close of the decade. Other talented novelists and poets such as Jean Toomer, Countee Cullen, and Nella Larsen virtually stopped writing. Still others, such as Arna Bontemps and Sterling Brown, turned to literary criticism and away from poetry and fiction-writing.

Other giants of the Renaissance drifted away from the philosophical roots of the movement, which had been based on racial self-exploration and ethnic pride. Langston Hughes embraced Communism and his writing increasingly emphasized other political and social themes. W.E.B. Du Bois, stung by years of criticism from younger writers who felt that he was too moralistic and uptight, left the NAACP in 1934, renounced the "New Negro Renaissance," and offered controversial support for the socialist

Soviet Union during the early years of the Cold War. Du Bois was also one of many leading Harlemites—along with James Weldon Johnson, Charles S. Johnson, Arthur Schomburg, Jessie Fauset, Aaron Douglas, and others—who left New York City in the late 1920s and 1930s.

Finally, the new generation of talented black writers to emerge in the 1930s and 1940s did not consciously identify themselves with the Harlem Renaissance. Ralph Ellison, Richard Wright, William Attaway, and others expressed profound respect for the works of their predecessors. Like those earlier writers, they also wrote about what it was like to be a black person in America. But they staked out new stylistic and thematic areas to explore as well, and they did not make their homes in Harlem.

Some architects of the Harlem Renaissance looked upon the crumbling literary foundations of the Renaissance with undisguised sadness. They felt that the movement was fading due to the selfish pursuit of pleasure, fame, and fortune, and that political goals such as racial equality had been forgotten. "Are we then in a period of cultural depression, verging on spiritual bankruptcy?" wrote Alain Locke in 1931:

African-American writers that rose to prominence during the 1940s, such as Richard Wright, were not closely associated with Harlem or the Renaissance era.

> Has the afflatus of Negro self-expression died down? Are we outliving the Negro fad? Has the Negro creative artist wandered into the ambush of the professional exploiters? By some signs and symptoms. Yes. . . . The second and truly sound phase of cultural development of the Negro in American literature and art cannot begin without a collapse of the boom, a change to more responsible and devoted leadership, a revision of basic values, and . . . a wholesale expulsion of the moneychangers from the temples of art.

The Trials of the Scottsboro Boys

During the 1930s, Black Harlemites—and much of the rest of the nation—developed an intense interest in a notorious rape case in Alabama in which a group of black youths were accused of raping two white women. The saga of the "Scottsboro Nine," as the defendants came to be known, stretched out for most of the decade. By the time it ended, it had become one of the most notorious legal cases in American history—and a vivid symbol of bigotry and racial inequality in the Jim Crow South.

In March 1931, nine young black males—the youngest of whom was only twelve years old—were falsely accused of gang-raping two white women on a freight train near Scottsboro, Alabama. During the first trials (the youths were tried in groups of two or three), the defendants were victimized by incompetent defense attorneys and blatantly racist jurors and judge. When the first series of trials concluded, eight of the nine Scottsboro Boys had been convicted and sentenced to death (a mistrial was declared in the case of twelve-year-old Roy Wright, when eleven jurors who wanted the death penalty failed to convince a lone juror who held out for a life sentence).

The trials of the Scottsboro Nine, though, were so riddled with legal problems that the cases were appealed all the way to the U.S. Supreme Court. In 1933 the Court overturned the convictions in the landmark case of *Powell vs. Alabama*, ruling by a 7-2 vote that the youths had been denied competent legal counsel and were thus entitled to new trials.

As preparations for new trials got underway, the case dominated headlines across the country. The defendants received occasional visits from well-known black supporters such as Langston Hughes, who penned *Scottsboro Limited: Four Poems and a Play in Verse* (1932) to publicize their plight. But they spent most of their time alone in horrible Depression-era state prisons. The first Scottsboro defendant to be re-tried in the spring of 1933 was Haywood Patterson. The all-white jury convicted Patterson and sentenced him to death, but Judge James Horton was so outraged by the verdict and sentence that he set them aside and ordered a new trial.

Over the next three years Patterson and defendant Clarence Norris became the focus of titanic legal battles. Both young men were convicted and sentenced to death yet again, only to have new trials ordered by higher courts. Patterson's fourth trial ended in 1936 with a conviction and seventy-five-year jail sentence. Norris, meanwhile, prepared for his third trial while the other seven black youths continued to languish in prison.

By 1937 seven of the nine Scottsboro defendants had been held in jail for over six years without trial. That year, Norris and three other defendants were convicted; they received sentences ranging from death to seventy-five years. They joined Patterson in the Alabama prison system. The remaining four Scottsboro Boys were abruptly released, with all charges dropped. This stunning turn of events is believed to have been part of a grim compromise between state prosecutors, who knew that the case had badly stained Alabama's reputation, and desperate defense attorneys.

For the five convicted members of the Scottsboro Nine, the next several years were nightmares. "They struggled with life in hellholes of prisons," wrote historian Douglas O. Linder. "Atmore Prison, near Mobile, was a desperate place teeming with poisonous snakes, sadistic guards, and rapacious prisoners. . . . They sodomized or were sodomized; they assaulted or were assaulted. They survived, but barely."

By 1950 all the Scottsboro Boys convicted in the rape case were out of prison. Charles Weems was paroled in 1943, Clarence Norris and Ozie Powell were released in 1946, and Andy Wright gained his freedom in 1950. Haywood Patterson escaped from prison in 1948. He was captured by the FBI in Michigan two years later, but Michigan's governor refused Alabama's demand for extradition. This did not constitute a happy ending for the Scottsboro Boys, however. By the time the ordeal was over, all of the defendants were impoverished and scarred from years of brutal experiences. Violence swirled around many of them long after the Scottsboro case faded from the nation's consciousness. The last of the Scottsboro Boys, Clarence Norris, died on January 23, 1989.

Sources:

Goodman, James E. *Stories of Scottsboro.* New York: Vintage, 1995.

Linder, Douglas O. "The Trials of 'The Scottsboro Boys.'" *Famous American Trials.* Available online at http://www.law.umkc.edu/faculty/projects/FTrials/scottsboro/scottsb.htm (accessed August 2007).

Injured rioters await transport to police headquarters after being arrested for their involvement in the Harlem Riot of 1935.

The Harlem Riot of 1935

Harlem's fraying reputation as the center of African-American literary, economic, and cultural activity was finally shattered in the early spring of 1935, when a violent race riot tore through the streets of the community. The riot erupted on March 19, after a young Puerto Rican man was arrested for shoplifting after a brief scuffle. An unfounded rumor that white police had beaten a black boy to death for shoplifting swept through the neighborhood. To many poor black residents, the tale of brutal white policemen was all too believable. A crowd formed outside some white-owned businesses that were notorious in the community for practicing racial discrimination. When a member of the mob smashed a store window in anger, the act triggered a long night of violence and looting. In his account of the riot for the *Nation*, Renaissance writer Claude McKay stated that "the crowds went crazy like the remnants of a defeated, abandoned, and hungry army. Their rioting was the gesture of despair of a bewildered, baffled, and disillusioned people."

On the morning of March 20, the sun rose over a broken community. Three African Americans were dead, dozens more had been arrested, two hundred stores had been burned and vandalized, and an estimated $2 million worth of property damage had been caused by the rioters. Even worse, the violence had shredded the Jazz Age reputation of the community as a glamorous cabaret of dancing, singing, and revelry. It had shown the rest of the world that the Harlem of the 1930s was a ghetto crowded with angry and exploited people at the bottom of America's socioeconomic ladder.

In the aftermath of the violence, community leaders set about tending Harlem's many wounds. Proud and hardy residents vowed to restore the neighborhood as well. These efforts enabled some of Harlem's remaining historic clubs, like the Savoy Ballroom, to stay in business. But the riot destroyed Harlem's fading claim that it was America's black metropolis. Leading African-American writers, artists, and intellectuals ceased to see the community as a gathering place for inspiration. "In the future, other African American writers would live and work in Harlem, but Harlem would never again be the center of a literary movement," wrote historian Cary D. Wintz in *Remembering the Harlem Renaissance*. "Harlem would never again be the African American symbol of progress and hope."

pillars of American society. "The Harlem Renaissance, with its ideological invitations to interracial problem solving, had long-lasting repercussions on American race relations well into mid-century and later," asserted historian Richard Powell.

The artistic triumphs of the Renaissance also boosted the self-esteem and self-awareness of black Americans. The exploits of the movement's painters, musicians, and writers gave African Americans greater confidence in their own capacity to force social change. In addition, their accomplishments bestowed upon them a deeper conviction that they truly deserved an equal role in American society. In addition, it led black Americans to embrace and celebrate their African roots, an important psychological development that remains a source of strength in African-American communities today.

The wonderful music and literature and art of the Renaissance era also contributed to the hardy character of the legal and political activists of the 1930s and 1940s. These men and women refused to abandon their dreams of racial equality despite setback after setback. And although bigotry remained rampant in white communities across America, the integrationist message of black activists resonated with growing numbers of whites as well. These whites had, by virtue of the Harlem Renaissance, gained a heightened understanding of the historical contributions that black Americans had made to their country—and increased awareness of their potential for making even greater contributions to American society if they were given access to the same educational, social, and financial tools that were available to their white countrymen.

Still, some observers point out that some of the most ambitious dreams that drove the Harlem Renaissance failed to materialize. For example, racial prejudice and ethnic divisions remained major problems not only in New York City, but all across America (see "Dorothy West Recalls Amateur Night at the Apollo Theatre," p. 190). "Part of the energy that fueled the Harlem Renaissance was the belief that black cultural achievement in the 'high' arts would socially and spiritually uplift the race," wrote Stuart. "Manifestly this has not happened. . . . Great novels may have come from Harlem, but how many living there now can read them?"

Other scholars, however, argue that the legacy of the Harlem Renaissance should not be discounted just because the movement failed to produce enduring racial equality in every facet of American life, as its leading architects had hoped. "While the movement—like most artistic movements—could not achieve its most ambitious social aims, it was nonetheless a turning point in

American cultural history," contended George Hutchinson in *The Harlem Renaissance in Black and White*. These defenders assert, for example, that the Civil Rights Movement of the 1950s and 1960s, which led to the passage of important federal laws against segregation and discrimination, might never have come to pass were it not for the political, social, and cultural activity stirred up by the Harlem Renaissance.

The Artistic Legacy of the Renaissance

Whereas the political impact of the Harlem Renaissance is open to debate, few dispute that the movement had an enormous and lasting impact on African-American literature, music, painting, sculpture, filmmaking, and other creative arts (see "Langston Hughes Remembers the Harlem Renaissance," p. 196). The Renaissance, wrote Stuart, "created a flowering of black talent that has left an ineradicable cultural legacy."

The Civil Rights Movement of the 1950s and 1960s led by Martin Luther King Jr. and other black leaders might never have come to pass were it not for the political activism of the Harlem Renaissance.

Importantly, this talent also made its presence felt well beyond the borders of black America. The works of Langston Hughes, Louis Armstrong, Countee Cullen, Zora Neale Hurston, Aaron Douglas, Paul Robeson, and countless other gifted black writers and artists changed the cultural fabric of *all* of America. As scholar David Levering Lewis wrote in *The Portable Harlem Renaissance Reader*, "mainstream America was [made] richer for the color, emotion, humanity, and cautionary vision produced by Harlem during its golden age."

Modern African-American artists as varied as filmmaker Spike Lee, playwright August Wilson, jazz legend Wynton Marsalis, and writer Maya Angelou have all cited the Harlem Renaissance as an enormously influential

This famous 1958 photograph by Art Kane gathered together Harlem's greatest jazz and blues musicians and composers for a group portrait.

and inspirational factor in the development of their own careers and artistic vision. Perhaps most importantly, the sculptors, painters, performers, and poets of the Renaissance "contributed the sense that for the first time the Black artist could take control of the images of Black America," declared Mary Schmidt Campbell in *Harlem Renaissance: Art of Black America.*

The celebration of African-American identity and heritage took many forms. Some leaders of the Renaissance, such as author Zora Neale Hurston and painter William H. Johnson, embraced autobiographies and self-portraits—forms of expression that today can be seen in the works of modern African-American artists like Spike Lee and Maya Angelou. Other Renaissance artists chose to explore the epic struggle for equality waged by black people throughout history. These works, such as the multi-paneled paintings of Jacob Lawrence and James Weldon Johnson's *Black Manhattan,* paved the way, decades later, for epic works such as Alex Haley's *Roots*, Toni Morrison's *Beloved*, and August Wilson's "Pittsburgh Cycle" of dramatic plays about the black experience in twentieth-century America. Other themes and artistic approaches that are commonplace among today's black artists and writers can be traced back to the Renaissance as well.

Today, the African-American artistic community is firmly integrated into the fabric of the larger U.S. and international communities. African-American musicians, singers, dance troupes, and stage actors routinely perform works by black composers and writers before ethnically diverse audiences. At the same time, though, America's black community has developed parallel institutions that are explicitly reserved to celebrate, recognize, and support African-American artists. For example, the works of numerous black sculptors, painters, filmmakers, and other artists are prominently featured in major art muse-

Spike Lee is one of many black filmmakers who have made lasting contributions to American cinema.

ums across the United States, but there also exist museums devoted exclusively to African and African-American artists of the past and present.

The Renaissance and Modern Black Literature

In terms of black culture, the Harlem Renaissance probably had a greater impact on African-American literature than any other form of artistic expression. "The mere fact that during the Renaissance black writers published with major firms and that white critics took their work seriously made things easier for the next generation," wrote Cary D. Wintz in *Black Culture and the Harlem Renaissance*. "Publishers and editors who had once routinely dismissed manuscripts by black authors no longer placed strict racial restrictions on what they published."

Langston Hughes, who became the most popular and critically acclaimed of all the writers of the movement, agreed that the Renaissance opened previously locked doors for future generations of black writers and artists. "When I

Beloved author Toni Morrison is one of the most acclaimed novelists in America today.

first started writing it was said that the *Saturday Evening Post* would not accept works written by Negroes," he recalled in his autobiography, *The Big Sea.* "Whether or not the *Post* actually followed such a policy, it did seem to be true of certain other magazines. . . . It can hardly be disputed that the 'Renaissance' did a great deal to make possible a public willing to accept Negro problems and Negro Art."

The novels, poems, essays, and short stories that came out of the Harlem Renaissance failed to eradicate all traces of racism and discrimination in the publishing world, of course. Numerous white editors and agents still felt free to express bigoted attitudes toward black writers during the 1940s and 1950s. During these same decades, blacks were rarely hired on to the editorial staffs of publishers, periodicals, or newspapers. Similarly, blacks were almost never given the opportunity to write book or theater reviews. The television industry was particularly slow to admit African-American screenwriters to its ranks; black faces were rarities on production teams (and on screen) until the 1970s.

Nonetheless, black authors such as Richard Wright, James Baldwin, and Ralph Ellison created some of the most important and powerful literary works of the 1940s and 1950s, and in 1950 Gwendolyn Brooks became the first African American to receive a Pulitzer Prize, for her 1950 poetry collection *Annie Allen.* White racism simply could not smother the enormous talents of these and other African-American writers.

Over time, the worlds of publishing and entertainment became fully integrated. Today, many African-Americans enjoy thriving careers as writers, editors, journalists, screenwriters, and playwrights. In addition, black writers have earned many of America's major literary prizes. Pulitzer Prize winners of the last two decades of the twentieth century included playwright August Wilson (for *Fences* in 1987 and *The Piano Lesson* in 1990) and novelist Toni Morrison (for *Beloved* in 1988). Morrison also received the Nobel Prize for Literature in 1993. Brooks (1985-86) and Rita Dove (1993-95) have served as poets laureate of the United States.

None of these prominent African-American writers would have been able to create the enduring literary works for which they are known if the Harlem Renaissance had not occurred. The writers of the Renaissance not only paved the way for broad public acceptance of black literature, they also carved out a powerful artistic path for future generations to explore. "The Harlem Renaissance was a success," wrote Wintz, "[because black writers] wanted to give expression to the black experience—to write about life as they saw it and to look deeply into the black race's existence in America. This they accomplished."

Harlem in the Twenty-First Century

The neighborhood of Harlem has undergone an economic renaissance of its own in the opening years of the twenty-first century. Throughout much of the second half of the twentieth century, the name "Harlem" was virtually synonymous with "ghetto." The problems with crime and poverty that riddled the community in the 1930s became even worse in ensuing decades. By the 1950s, Harlem had become entrenched as one of the most notorious ghettos in all of America. A handful of historic churches and entertainment venues were the community's only links to its glorious Jazz Age past.

Beginning in the 1960s, several efforts to revitalize Harlem were launched, but none of these urban renewal projects stemmed the general sense of decline and decay afflicting the community. Race riots brought on by deplorable living conditions and economic hopelessness rocked the community in the 1960s and 1970s. Harlem's dedicated core of community activists, entrepreneurs, and concerned citizens suffered further setbacks in the 1980s, when AIDS and a crack cocaine epidemic swept across America. These problems affected all races and regions of the country, but they were particularly devastating to Harlem and other poor urban communities that did not have the educational, health, or financial resources to mount an effective defense.

Even in these darkest days, however, neighborhood churches and other community organizations cooperated with public and private institutions to keep Harlem alive. They built playgrounds and gardens in blighted areas, nurtured children's programs, and established community programs in the areas of job skills, health care, and education—including a number of parochial, African-centered, and community-chartered schools.

This refusal to succumb to despair paid off in the 1990s, when a robust national economy triggered increased investment in Harlem. After the Upper

The Legacy of Oscar Micheaux

When asked to cite influences and inspirations in their own work, many contemporary African-American filmmakers quickly offer up the name of Oscar Micheaux. Born on January 2, 1884, in Metropolis, Illinois, Micheaux grew up to become the first African American to direct, write, and produce a feature-length motion picture.

Micheaux first worked as a farm laborer, railroad porter, and homesteading farmer in South Dakota, but in the mid-1910s he became both a novelist and a filmmaker. His first novel, *The Conquest* (1913), was a semi-autobiographical story about a black homesteader in the Midwest. He wrote six other novels over the course of his lifetime, the most successful of which was *The Case of Mrs. Wingate* (1945).

Micheaux's chief artistic legacy, though, is as a filmmaker. He first made a name for himself in the silent film era with *The Homesteaders* (1919), but it was *Within Our Gates* (1920) for which he is best known. *Within Our Gates* was in many ways a response to *Birth of a Nation,* a famous and wildly popular 1915 film by D.W. Griffith that portrayed blacks in an extremely demeaning and negative light. Micheaux's movie turned the tables by portraying blacks in positive ways and showing whites in unflattering lights.

Over the next three decades Micheaux produced, directed, and wrote at least 43 films (27 silent films and 16 films with sound). His 1931 film *The*

Manhattan Empowerment Zone was established by the Clinton administration in 1994, $300 million in federal, state, and city funds poured into Harlem to create new businesses and jobs. Economic growth followed, and talk of a second Harlem "renaissance" began to be heard throughout the community. The sense of rebirth surrounding Harlem intensified in 2001, when former President Bill Clinton established his offices there.

Modern Harlem still has significant problems. Some areas of Harlem still lack supermarkets, restaurants, dry cleaners, and other businesses. Long-time residents and business owners with limited financial resources are finding it

Exile was the first American "talkie" movie to be produced by a black person. Notable actors ranging from Paul Robeson to Robert Earl Jones (father of actor James Earl Jones) also appeared in his films. Some of his films are today regarded as sexually racy, but he also tackled important subjects such as interracial relationships, bigotry within the black community based on skin coloration, and lynching and other white-on-black violence.

Micheaux died of a heart attack on March 25, 1951, in Charlotte, North Carolina. More than a half-century later, Spike Lee, Carl Franklin, Robert Townsend, and other African-American film directors and producers all hail Micheaux as a pioneering figure in black cinema. The Black Film Center/Archive bestows an annual Oscar Micheaux Distinguished Achievement Award to honor the links between recipients and the history and tradition of black filmmakers who have preceded them. Other awards bestowed in Micheaux's name are handed out by such notable film organizations as the Directors Guild of America, the Producers Guild of America, and the Black Filmmakers Hall of Fame.

Sources:

Bowser, Pearl, and Louis Spence. *Writing Himself into History: Oscar Micheaux, His Silent Films, and His Audiences.* New Brunswick, NJ: Rutgers University Press, 2000.

Green, Ronald J. *Straight Lick: The Cinema of Oscar Micheaux.* Bloomington, IN: Indiana University Press, 2000.

difficult to keep up with rising rents and other expenses. Crime, drug abuse, and high drop-out rates continue to hamper the neighborhood. Some observers also worry that gentrification threatens Harlem's cultural history and vitality.

The community, though, also enjoys greater economic vitality now than it has at any time since the height of the Harlem Renaissance. Clubs that have been closed for years have reopened, new restaurants are flocking to West Harlem, neglected buildings are being renovated as condominiums, and historic churches such as the Riverside Church, the Abyssinian Baptist Church,

In 2001 former President Bill Clinton (center) established his business headquarters in Harlem.

Salem United Methodist Church, and Metropolitan Baptist Church remain stalwart members of the community. These developments are encouraging to Americans—black and white—who would like nothing more than for Harlem to reclaim its former standing as one of America's most exciting, vibrant, and culturally significant communities.

BIOGRAPHIES

Aaron Douglas (1899-1979)
Painter and Illustrator of the Harlem Renaissance

Photographed by Carl Van Vechten.

Aaron Douglas was born in Topeka, Kansas, on May 26, 1899. His parents, Aaron Sr. and Elizabeth, had migrated to the Great Plains from the Deep South during the post-Reconstruction era. One of Douglas's earliest artistic influences was his mother, who enjoyed drawing and painting during the precious few hours when she was not caring for her children or attending to household chores.

By the time Douglas graduated from Topeka High School in 1917, he had already developed into a promising young artist. Restless to make his mark in the world, he cast his gaze to the industrial cities to the east, where he hoped to earn money to continue his education. "Detroit, the money Mecca of every young Negro youth who yearned to escape the oppressive conditions of his life, was the place where my journey came to a temporary halt," he recalled years later in an unpublished autobiography.

Douglas worked in Detroit's exploding automobile industry for several months. Shrugging off his weariness at the end of his long shifts, he filled his evenings by attending free art classes at the Detroit Museum of Art (now the Detroit Institute of Art). His factory work experiences in Detroit, though brief, had a lasting impact on his art. The pride and determination of fellow black laborers inspired him and contributed to his later depictions of African-American workers as strong and noble figures.

The Siren Call of the Harlem Renaissance

After he had saved enough money to resume his schooling, Douglas enrolled at the University of Nebraska in Lincoln in 1918. He was one of the only black students in the entire university, but he earned the grudging respect of fellow students and faculty with his talent and passion for art. After earning his bachelor's degree in fine arts from Nebraska in 1922, he

97

spent the next few years teaching art at Lincoln High School in Kansas City, Missouri.

During his years in Lincoln and Kansas City, Douglas displayed a growing fascination with the early stirrings of the Harlem Renaissance, the Negro political, cultural, and literary movement that was at that time transforming New York City. Douglas's own thirst to see racial equality in America had been deepened during World War I, when a racist officer in Nebraskas rejected his efforts to volunteer for military service in 1917 solely because of the color of his skin. The memory of this humiliation made it even easier for Douglas to embrace the declarations of racial pride expressed by W.E.B. Du Bois, Langston Hughes, James Weldon Johnson, and other luminaries of the Renaissance.

In the spring of 1925 Douglas's world was rocked by the publication of a special issue of *Survey Graphic* magazine that was devoted to Harlem and its foremost civil rights leaders, writers, and artists. Inspired by the publication's descriptions of Harlem as a vibrant black community with a thriving, exciting artistic and literary scene, Douglas left the security of his teaching position behind to see this "Negro Mecca" of America for himself.

The "Prodigal Son" of the Renaissance

After his arrival in Harlem in the summer of 1925, Douglas was introduced to Du Bois, whose many activities at that time included editorship of *The Crisis,* the literary magazine of the National Association for the Advancement of Colored People (NAACP). Douglas also met Charles S. Johnson, the influential editor of *Opportunity,* the magazine of the National Urban League (NUL).

Another important encounter was with Rinold Weiss, the European artist who had provided the Africa-inspired cover art for the special Harlem issue of *Survey Graphic.* When Weiss offered Douglas a scholarship to study in his private studio, the young Kansas native quickly accepted. He spent the next several months soaking up knowledge from Weiss and studying African art in various private and public collections scattered throughout New York City.

Both Johnson and Du Bois were impressed by the young artist's potential, and in 1926 they commissioned him to provide cover and interior illustrations for both *Opportunity* and *Crisis.* In addition, Alain Locke hired him to provide illustrations for *The New Negro,* an expanded book-sized version of the *Survey Graphic* issue on the Harlem Renaissance.

Douglas's work surpassed even the most optimistic hopes of these early clients, all of whom were giants of the Renaissance. His illustrations blended an arresting visual style of flat forms and hard geometric shapes with images taken both from ancient African culture and contemporary African-American life. The final result was a bold, striking vision of the modern black American spirit. "As I remember now, [my early illustrations] were gladly received with no questions asked," Douglas later said. "They seemed to have been in a miraculous way a heaven-sent answer to some deeply felt need for this kind of visual imagery. As a result, I became a kind of fair-haired boy and was treated in some ways as a prodigal son. I began to feel like the missing piece that all had been looking for to complete or round out the idea of the Renaissance."

Triumph and Rebellion

In 1926 Douglas married Alta Mae Sawyer, a former high school sweetheart who left an unhappy marriage to be with the artist. Their Harlem home became one of the most popular and stimulating gathering spots among the community's top young writers and artists.

During this time, Douglas and many of the poets and painters with whom he socialized expressed rising impatience with black civil rights leaders and liberal white supporters. They felt that these activists and patrons wanted them to produce works that advanced the cause of racial equality at the expense of their own artistic desires and explorations. Determined to establish his artistic independence, Douglas broke ties with the wealthy white socialite Charlotte Osgood Mason, one of his main financial patrons. Other young writers and artists took similar steps to proclaim their determination to explore all facets of black life in America.

In 1926 Wallace Thurman organized Douglas and several other of these Renaissance rebels to produce a radical new black literary magazine called *Fire!!* Douglas contributed several powerful illustrations to the publication, which he saw as a sign of a dawning new age in black art and literature. "We have no axes to grind," Douglas declared. "[But] we believe that the Negro is fundamentally, essentially different from their Nordic neighbors. We are proud of that difference. We believe these differences to be greater spiritual endowment, greater sensitivity, greater power for artistic expression and appreciation. We believe Negro art should be trained and developed rather than capitalized and exploited." As it turned out, only one issue of the magazine was ever published before financial problems killed it. Years later, though, Douglas expressed great pride in the magazine and the defiant spirit of its creators.

Douglas's work for *Fire!!* further cemented his reputation as the leading visual spokesman for the Harlem Renaissance. By the late 1920s his highly symbolic drawings and paintings had become synonymous in the minds of many with the boldest elements of the movement. "Aaron Douglas drawing strange black fantasies causes the smug Negro middle class to turn from their white, respectable, ordinary books and papers to catch a glimpse of their own beauty," declared poet Langston Hughes, one of Douglas's closest friends.

Turning to Murals

Douglas added to his artistic legacy in the late 1920s with some of his most enduring book and journal illustrations. Notable works of this type included illustrations for Thurman's *The Blacker the Berry* (1929) and Paul Morand's *Black Magic* (1929). His most famous illustrations, though, appeared in James Weldon Johnson's 1927 masterwork *God's Trombones: Seven Negro Sermons in Verse.* In this book, wrote Renaissance scholar George Hutchinson, "Douglas transformed traditional white Christian iconography by putting black subjects in central roles and evoking (like Johnson's poems) the identification of black Americans with the suffering of Jesus and other central motifs of the Bible. His stylized, silhouette-like renderings of Negro physical features, imbued with qualities of both spiritual yearning and implicit dignity, became a signature of the movement."

In 1930 Douglas went to Fisk University, a black school in Nashville, Tennessee, to tackle a new artistic challenge: mural painting. As artist in residence, he painted a cycle of murals for the university's new library. Collectively, these murals provided a tapestry of black triumphs and tragedies through history.

In 1931 Douglas and his wife traveled to France. He spent more than a year studying in Paris, where he also met Henry Ossawa Tanner and many other expatriate black artists and entertainers. They returned to Harlem in the summer of 1932 and settled in a new home in the community's prosperous Sugar Hill area. The following year Douglas had his first solo exhibition, at Caz Delbo Gallery in New York.

In 1934, the Works Progress Administration (WPA) commissioned Douglas to paint *Aspects of Negro Life,* a four-panel mural for the Harlem branch of the New York Public Library on 135th street. This cycle of panels—*The Negro in an African Setting, Slavery Through Reconstruction, An Idyll of the Deep South,* and *Song of the Towers*—remain Douglas's most famous mural works. Using powerful imagery from Africa, the Deep South, and twentieth-century America, Douglas chronicled African-American history from ancient times to the industrial age. Today, this mural cycle is housed at the Schomburg Center for Research in Black Culture in Harlem.

Douglas spent much of the next few years working on murals from New York City to Dallas. He also served as the first president of the Harlem Artists' Guild, founded in 1935. As president, he successfully lobbied WPA administrators to give greater numbers of commissions to black artists struggling to make ends meet in Depression-era America.

Return to Fisk

In 1937 Douglas returned to Fisk University to become the founding chairman of the school's art department. He stayed at Fisk for the next four decades, though he also traveled widely in Europe, Africa, and Latin America during these years. In 1944 he earned a master's degree in fine arts from Teacher's College at Columbia University.

Douglas retired from Fisk University in 1966, but he remained active. In 1969 he undertook a painstaking restoration of the murals he had painted for the Fisk library back in the 1930s. In some cases, Douglas actually repainted panels, using more bold and vibrant colors than in the original. After his restoration efforts, some of the murals were unfortunately lost, but the rest have been carefully restored and preserved. After his retirement, Douglas also frequently lectured on the history of African-American art and the Harlem Renaissance. He died in Nashville on February 3, 1979.

Today, Douglas continues to rank as the foremost visual artist of the Harlem Renaissance. "He recognized that he had a unique power as an artist," wrote Amy Helene Kirschke in *Harlem Speaks,* "and he was always willing to take risks to relay his message. Through his illustrations, murals, paintings, and teaching, Aaron Douglas inspired both the public and his students to explore and celebrate African American history and culture."

Sources:

Aaron Douglas: African American Modernist. Lawrence, KS: University of Kansas, Spencer Museum of Art, 2007.

Driskoll, David. *Harlem Renaissance: Art of Black Americans.* New York: Abrams, 1987.

Hutchinson, George. "The Harlem Renaissance," in *Encyclopedia of American Cultural and Intellectual History.* Edited by Mary Kupiec Cayton and Peter W. Williams. New York: Scribner's, 2001.

Kirschke, Amy Helene. *Aaron Douglas, Art, Race & The Harlem Renaissance.* Jackson: University Press of Mississippi, 1995.

Kirschke, Amy Helene. "Aaron Douglas," in *Harlem Speaks.* Edited by Cary D. Wintz. Naperville, IL: Sourcebooks, 2007.

W.E.B. Du Bois (1868-1963)
Author, Scholar, and Civil Rights Leader

William Edward Burroughs Du Bois was born in Great Barrington, Massachusetts, on February 23, 1868. His father was Alfred Du Bois, a Union Army veteran of mixed white and black ancestry who had been born in Haiti. His mother was Mary Silvina Burghardt Du Bois, a black woman. Du Bois's father abandoned the family when Du Bois was still a toddler. Several years later, his mother suffered a stroke and she and her son were forced to rely on relatives for financial support.

Du Bois was an excellent and ambitious student, and the community in which he grew up did not suffer from the awful levels of ugly racism that afflicted the American South. Still, he endured childhood insults and indignities solely because of his skin color. These incidents wounded him, but he responded with grit and defiance. By his own admission, he began to take great pleasure in outperforming his white peers, both on the playground and in the classroom.

A Foundation for Success

In 1885 Du Bois enrolled at Fisk College (now Fisk University), a black school in Nashville, Tennessee. This continuation of his education was only made possible by generous tuition assistance from four New England Congregational churches. During the next three years, he served as editor of the college newspaper and excelled in classes in literature, chemistry, physics, philosophy, and various foreign languages. Du Bois also spent two summers teaching black children in rural Tennessee. This summer work exposed him to the crippling economic and social conditions under which African Americans lived in the Jim Crow South. Du Bois was both outraged and moved by their plight, and it was during this period that he first began to envision a future for himself as a champion of black civil rights.

After graduating from Fisk with a bachelor's degree in 1888, Du Bois received a scholarship to attend Harvard University in Cambridge, Massachusetts. Studying history and philosophy, he earned a master's degree in 1892 and a fellowship to study for two years at the University of Berlin in Germany. After returning to the United States, he resumed his studies. In 1896 he became the first African American in Harvard's history to receive a doctorate degree. That same year he married Nina Gomer.

Du Bois briefly taught at Wilberforce University, a black school in Ohio, but late in 1896 he accepted an offer from the University of Pennsylvania to conduct a research study of the black population of the city of Philadelphia. Three years later, the results of his research were published as *The Philadelphia Negro*. This groundbreaking sociological study was the nation's first detailed analysis of an African-American community.

In 1899 Du Bois joined the faculty of Atlanta University in Georgia. He led the sociology department at the all-black school for the next decade. During this time he gained a reputation as a demanding instructor and a tireless investigator of all facets of African-American life, from economic and health issues to the role of religion in family and community life. Du Bois's findings were incorporated into a series of reports collectively known as the Atlanta University Studies. Du Bois's efforts in this area reflected his early belief that social science research could be used to help America recognize and address its serious problems with discrimination and racism. But his findings were largely ignored by the white establishment, leading Du Bois to turn toward a more militant approach to combating America's "race problem."

A New Advocate for Black America

In 1903 the world learned that African Americans had a brilliant new spokesman in their midst, one who possessed a gift for writing as well as towering energy and intellect. It was in this year that Du Bois published *The Souls of Black Folk*, a collection of essays about American race relations and the black experience in the United States. This masterpiece eloquently explained what life was like for black Americans trapped behind the nation's "veil" of segregation and exclusion. *The Souls of Black Folk* also proclaimed the author's fierce conviction that blacks deserved full social equality in accordance with America's stated ideals. "We have woven ourselves with the very warp and woof of this nation," Du Bois wrote:

> We have fought their battles, shared their sorrow, mingled our
> blood with theirs, and generation after generation have plead-

ed with a headstrong, careless people to despise not Justice, Mercy and Truth, lest the nation be smitten with a curse. Our song, our toil, our cheer and warning have been given to this nation in blood brotherhood. Are not these gifts worth the giving? Is not this worth the striving? Would America have been America without her Negro People?

That same year, Du Bois published an essay titled "The Talented Tenth." In this work he insisted that black advancement in America depended on educational opportunity. He also called on America's small number of educated and prosperous blacks, the so-called Talented Tenth, to lead the fight for social equality. "The Negro race, like all races, is going to be saved by its exceptional men," he stated. "The problem of education, then, among Negroes must first of all deal with the Talented Tenth; it is the problem of developing the Best of this race that they may guide the Mass away from the contamination and death of the Worst, in their own and other races."

Du Bois's words had a major impact within the black community and among liberal white supporters of the African-American struggle for equality. But they also posed a direct challenge to Booker T. Washington, the nation's best-known advocate for African Americans. Washington had long pursued a course of racial advancement that focused on vocational training and economic self-sufficiency rather than social equality. Du Bois's words made it clear that he did not agree with this philosophy, and from this point forward the two men waged an ongoing battle of ideas.

The Niagara Movement and the NAACP

In 1905 Du Bois helped organize a historic meeting of two dozen black leaders on the Canadian side of Niagara Falls. This group, which came to be known as the Niagara Movement, emerged from the meeting with a historic "Declaration of Principles" that condemned racial discrimination and segregation in American society. The Niagara Movement only lasted a few years before disbanding, but it became the foundation for the 1909 birth of the National Association for the Advancement of Colored People (NAACP), the most important civil rights organization in American history.

In 1910 Du Bois became the founding editor of *The Crisis*, the flagship magazine of the NAACP. Under his guidance, *The Crisis* became a major outlet for talented African-American writers and poets, especially during the early years of the Harlem Renaissance. It also became a vehicle for Du Bois to issue his own fearless condemnations of white racism and inspirational messages of black dignity and hope. Under Du Bois's direction, "scholarship, racial propaganda, visionary pronouncements, and majestic indignation thundered and flashed [from *The Crisis*] across Afro-America and beyond for a quarter of a century," wrote historian David Levering Lewis in *W.E.B. Du Bois: Biography of a Race.*

Du Bois spread his message in other ways as well. In 1912 he published his first novel, *The Quest of the Silver Fleece,* which dramatized the black struggle to triumph over the rampant racism afflicting American society. Three years later he published *The Negro,* a history of blacks in Africa and around the world. And in 1920, just as the Harlem Renaissance was emerging as a major cultural force in America, he published a collection of essays called *Darkwater: Voices from within the Veil.* In this work, he urged African Americans to stand strong in the face of adversity and proclaimed his belief in the common humanity of all peoples. "I believe in God who made of one blood all nations that on earth do dwell," he stated. "I believe that all men, black and brown and white, are brothers, varying through time and opportunity, in form and gift and feature, but differing in no essential particular, and alike in soul and the possibility of infinite development."

Du Bois's passion for civil rights and his quest for knowledge led him in other directions as well. In 1919 he organized the first of several "Pan-African" congresses in which he participated over the years. These conferences, which attracted an international roster of black intellectuals and activists, were devoted to improving the lives of people of African descent around the globe. In 1924 he traveled to Africa for the first time.

Disillusionment with the Harlem Renaissance

During the first years of the Harlem Renaissance, Du Bois expressed great excitement about its potential for advancing the civil rights cause. Du Bois believed that the art and literature being produced by blacks proved that they were just as artistically gifted as whites. He further asserted that if the movement's paintings, poems, music, and novels portrayed African Americans as a noble and dignified people, they might be an effective weapon against white bigotry and ignorance.

In the mid-1920s, though, Du Bois voiced mounting frustration with the literary and artistic work being produced by leading individuals of the Harlem Renaissance. Langston Hughes, Claude McKay, and other prominent members of the movement insisted on full artistic independence to explore all facets of black life—including the frailties, frustrations, and flaws of African Americans. Du Bois saw this stance as selfish and shortsighted, especially since they were living in an era when segregation remained rampant, anti-black violence was commonplace, and the Ku Klux Klan was surging in popularity in many northern cities. By the late 1920s, Du Bois had abandoned his role as promoter of the Harlem Renaissance. Instead, he became one of the most influential and persistent critics of the movement inside America's black community.

A New Start in Atlanta

In 1928 Du Bois published *The Dark Princess,* a novel that is often described as a work of the Harlem Renaissance. But even as this book was being snapped off bookstore shelves, many of Du Bois's editorials and essays suggested the author's growing interest in the economic roots of class division and in socialist political theory. This shift was undoubtedly due in part to a 1927 visit he paid to Communist Russia.

Du Bois remained an important figure in the nation's African American community in the 1930s. In 1932, for example, the NAACP awarded him the Springarn Medal for outstanding achievement by a black American. His increasingly vocal praise of socialism, though, upset many other members of the organization. In 1934 Du Bois resigned his editorship of *The Crisis* and left New York City to return to the faculty of Atlanta University.

In 1935 Du Bois published *Black Reconstruction* (1935), a scholarly work that explored the exploitation of black people in America and the rest of the world throughout history. A variety of other works followed, some of which touted racial separatism as a way to solve the country's ongoing racial strife. These works were condemned by NAACP officials and other black leaders. They charged that Du Bois was helping the cause of the Ku Klux Klan and other racists who asserted that blacks fared better under segregation.

After World War II Du Bois regularly made his presence felt on the international stage. In 1945 he rejoined the NAACP and served as part of a delegation that participated in the drafting of the charter for the newly founded

United Nations organization. That same year, he presided over the historic Manchester Pan-African Congress in England.

As the 1940s drew to a close, though, Du Bois clashed repeatedly with the U.S. government. He joined the left-wing American Labor Party and became a high-profile critic of American foreign policy during the early years of the Cold War. The federal government responded by branding him a "subversive" and Communist sympathizer. As government-sponsored harassment of Du Bois escalated, the NAACP revoked Du Bois's membership. The organization took this step out of a well-founded concern that enemies of their civil rights platform would use Du Bois to paint the entire organization as an agent of Communism, a political system that most Americans hated and feared.

In 1950 Du Bois's first wife, Nina Gomer, died after more than five decades of marriage. In February 1951 he married writer Shirley Graham. Over the next several years Du Bois continued to speak out against U.S. foreign policy and America's continued mistreatment of its black citizens. In 1958 the U.S. State Department lifted a seven-year foreign travel ban that it had imposed on Du Bois. He and his wife promptly went on an extended tour of the Soviet Union—where he received the Lenin International Peace Prize—and Africa.

In the early 1960s Du Bois and his wife moved to the African nation of Ghana. In 1963 he renounced his U.S. citizenship and became a citizen of Ghana. He also formally joined the Communist Party. He died on August 27, 1963, on the eve of the famed "March on Washington," one of the most famous events of the American civil rights movement.

Du Bois's Legacy

During the last three decades of his life, Du Bois's evolving political views put him out of step with much of the African-American civil rights mainstream. After his death, however, the nation's civil rights leadership rushed to pay tribute to the legendary activist, philosopher, and scholar. For example, *The Crisis,* the NAACP journal that Du Bois had edited for so many years, hailed its former editor as "the prime inspirer, philosopher, and father of the Negro protest movement."

Martin Luther King Jr., the single greatest leader of the American civil rights movement that swept across the nation in the 1960s, expressed similar sentiments about Du Bois. "History cannot ignore W.E.B. Du Bois because history has to reflect truth and Dr. Du Bois was a tireless explorer and a gifted discoverer of social truths," King wrote. "His singular greatness lay in his quest for truth about his own people. There were very few scholars who concerned themselves with honest study of the black man and he sought to fill this immense void. The degree to which he succeeded disclosed the great dimensions of the man."

Sources:

Du Bois, W.E.B. *The Oxford W.E.B. Du Bois Reader.* Edited by Eric J. Sundquist. New York: Oxford University Press, 1996.

Du Bois, W.E.B. *The Souls of Black Folk.* 1903. Reprint. New York: Penguin Classics, 1996.

Lewis, David Levering. *W.E.B. Du Bois: Biography of a Race, 1868-1919.* New York: Henry Holt, 1993.

Lewis, David Levering. *W.E.B. Du Bois: The Fight for Equality and the American Century, 1919-1963.* New York: Henry Holt, 2000.

Rampersad, Arnold. *The Art and Imagination of W.E.B. Du Bois.* Cambridge, MA: Harvard University Press, 1976.

Wintz, Cary D. *Black Culture and the Harlem Renaissance.* Houston: Rice University Press, 1988.

Duke Ellington (1899-1974)
Composer, Pianist, and Leader of the Duke Ellington Orchestra

Edward Kennedy "Duke" Ellington was born on April 29, 1899, in Washington, D.C. He was raised by his parents, Daisy Kennedy Ellington and James Edward Ellington, in segregated but comfortable black middle-class surroundings. His father worked as a butler, blueprint maker, and caterer at various times during his son's childhood. His income enabled him to raise "Duke"—a nickname he acquired from childhood friends—and his younger sister Ruth in a comfortable, nurturing environment.

Ellington began taking piano lessons around age seven, although he later acknowledged that he did not really develop a genuine passion for music until his teens. At that time, though, he became fascinated by blues and ragtime music. He began playing ragtime piano at cafes and parties around the capital, and in 1917 he dropped out of the vocational trade high school he was attending and formed his first band—Duke's Serenaders, Colored Syncopaters. In addition to his duties as pianist, Ellington also acted as the band's manager and publicist. In July 1918 he married Edna Thompson. They had a son, Mercer Kennedy Ellington, one year later.

Making His Mark in New York City

Ellington's band became a fixture at clubs and private parties around Washington and across the Potomac River in Virginia. Ellington's talent and ambition, however, led him to set his sights on New York City, where the first stirrings of the Harlem Renaissance were being felt.

In 1923 Ellington took his band, now known as the Washingtonians, to New York City. His initial efforts to stake out a place for himself and the band in the city's highly competitive music scene met only limited success, but he remained undaunted. Ellington made friends with respected veterans of New York's jazz scene, such as Paul Whiteman and Willie "the Lion" Smith, and the band made the most of the gigs they did get.

Late in 1923 Ellington was invited to join Elmer Snowden's Novelty Orchestra. He spent the next several months with the band, whose membership came to respect his musical ability and his classy demeanor. When the band learned in 1924 that Snowden had been cheating some members out of their fair share of earnings, they booted Snowden out of the band and installed Ellington as the new bandleader.

Over the next few years, Ellington and the Novelty Orchestra made Manhattan's Kentucky Club (originally known as the Hollywood Club) their primary home, though they played occasional dates all around the city and went on extensive summer tours. The popularity of the band—now known as the Kentucky Club Orchestra—soared to new heights during this time, boosted in part by a string of well-received records and in part by the deft management of Irving Mills, a veteran player in the New York music industry. Mills guided Ellington's orchestra from the mid-1920s until 1939, and during that time he organized tours, recording sessions, and promotional appearances that helped make Ellington the best-known jazz bandleader in the world.

Mills never would have been able to accomplish this feat, though, if Ellington had not put together a top-notch orchestra. Ellington insisted that the members of the band handle themselves responsibly and with discipline. Musicians who were late for rehearsals or recording sessions, or who let drinking interfere with their performance, did not last long. Equally important, Ellington composed wonderful musical arrangements that both challenged and rewarded the band. His music reflected the musical strengths and interests of individual band members. "You've got to write with certain men in mind," he explained. "You write just for their abilities and natural tendencies and give them places where they do their best."

Performing at the Cotton Club

In 1927 Ellington's band took the name "Duke Ellington Orchestra" and accepted an offer to become the house band for the Cotton Club, a prestigious but controversial club in the heart of Harlem. The Cotton Club employed African-American entertainers and waitstaff, but it only allowed white customers to enter its doors. The existence of this bastion of segregation in Harlem, the best-known black community in America, angered many African-Americans in New York. Ellington, though, used the gig to become the best-known bandleader in the country, white or black.

During his four years at the Cotton Club, Ellington composed a tremendous number of innovative and exciting songs. One of his most memorable trademarks was to use the voices of singers as additional musical instruments. Another was to embrace musical forms and sounds that had roots in ancient African music. "That's the pulse," he stated. "The African pulse. It's all the way back from what they first recognized as the old slave chants."

Ellington also attracted the finest musicians in New York to the Cotton Club. Famed jazz men such as baritone saxophonist Harry Carney, trumpeter Cootie Williams, trombonist Lawrence Brown, and alto saxophonist Johnny Hodges all joined the Duke Ellington Orchestra during the so-called "Cotton Club" years; all four were still performing with Ellington in the late 1960s.

Shortly after settling in at the Cotton Club, the Duke Ellington Orchestra was performing concerts that were broadcast live on national radio to all corners of the country. The music that crackled over the nation's radio waves captured the attention of music lovers everywhere, and by the close of the 1920s, these broadcasts had transformed Ellington into one of America's greatest stars.

King of Swing

In 1931 the Duke Ellington Orchestra parted ways with the Cotton Club and embarked on an ambitious and hugely successful world concert tour. The tour came at a fortunate time for Ellington, for it enabled him to leave New York just as the Harlem Renaissance was beginning its long and fitful decline. After Ellington's return to the United States, he displayed a great knack for adjusting to changing musical trends. In the early 1930s, for example, he rode the crest of the 1930s' swing music craze to further fame and fortune. The defining song of the era of swing—a form of jazz music that emphasizes fast tempo and a strong rhythm section—was Ellington's 1931 hit "It Don't Mean a Thing If It Ain't Got That Swing."

The Duke Ellington Orchestra remained atop the jazz world for the next several years. In 1939 composer Billy Strayhorn joined the band and immediately penned the famous song "Take the 'A' Train" for Ellington. Within a matter of months, Strayhorn became Ellington's chief collaborator. They composed music together for the next three decades, until Strayhorn's death in 1967.

The Duke Ellington Orchestra remained a top concert draw in the 1940s and early 1950s, and Ellington's love of music led him to explore new challenges, such as writing the 1941 all-black musical *Jump for Joy*. "Music is everything," he wrote. "Without music I may feel blind, atrophied, incomplete, *inexistent*." As time passed, however, Ellington became one of many victims of jazz's fading popularity with American audiences. His band remained popular, but it no longer enjoyed the popular or critical buzz that had surrounded it in the late 1920s and 1930s.

In 1956, though, Ellington signaled that he was still an exciting artist to be reckoned with. He and his orchestra delivered an electrifying performance at that year's Newport Jazz Festival, ushering in a grand new chapter in his career. A recording of the performance became the best-selling jazz album of the year and triggered a resurgence of interest in the jazz giant.

A Jazz Legend

During the 1950s and 1960s Ellington continued to compose all sorts of music, from motion picture scores to music pieces such as "What Color Is Virtue?—What Color Is Love?" that reflected the era's civil rights struggles. And from 1965 to 1973 he wrote three self-described "sacred concerts" that combined elements of jazz, Negro spirituals, classical music, gospel, blues, and choral music. These compositions, which Ellington described as the most important of his entire career, were played in churches and cathedrals all around the world.

The 1960s and early 1970s also brought Ellington the greatest honors of his illustrious career. He received eleven Grammy Awards and nineteen honorary degrees during his career. In 1969 he received the Presidential Medal of Freedom, the highest honor the U.S. government can bestow on an American civilian. Four years later, the French government awarded him the Legion of Honor, which is the highest honor France can give to a civilian.

In 1966 Edna Ellington, Ellington's wife of nearly five decades, passed away. In truth, however, they had long been married in name only. Ellington spent most of his adult life in the company of a succession of women, including a long relationship with Beatrice Ellis. As he admitted in his autobiography, however, the greatest love of his life was music: "I have a mistress. Lovers have come and gone, but only my mistress stays. She is beautiful and gentle. She waits on me hand and foot. She is a swinger. She has grace. To hear her speak, you can't believe your ears. She is ten thousand years old. . . . Music is my mistress, and she plays second fiddle to no one."

Ellington died of lung cancer and pneumonia on May 24, 1974, leaving behind a rich artistic legacy. He is remembered today as one of the giants of American entertainment, a visionary and influential jazz composer whose music remains immensely popular around the world.

Sources:

Ellington, Edward Kennedy. *Music Is My Mistress.* Cambridge, MA: Da Capo Press, 1976.

Hasse, John Edward. *Beyond Category: The Life and Genius of Duke Ellington.* Cambridge, MA: Da Capo Press, 1995.

Tucker, Mark. *The Duke Ellington Reader.* New York: Oxford University Press, 1993.

Langston Hughes (1902-1967)
Playwright, Novelist, and "Poet Laureate" of the Harlem Renaissance

James Langston Hughes was born in Joplin, Missouri, on February 1, 1902. His mother, Carrie Mercer Hughes, and his father, James Hughes, divorced when he was a small child. Langston's mother struggled to provide financial support for her son. As a result, he spent most of his childhood in Lawrence, Kansas, in the care of his maternal grandmother, Mary Langston, the first black woman to graduate from Ohio's Oberlin College.

After his grandmother's death in 1915, Hughes moved to Lincoln, Illinois, to live with his mother and her husband. One year later, the family moved to Cleveland, Ohio, where Hughes attended high school. Popular and outgoing, he graduated in 1920 with a thirst for knowledge and literature that had been kindled by writers such as black poet Paul Laurence Dunbar and French novelist Guy de Maupassant. W.E.B. Du Bois's famous essay collection *The Souls of Black Folk* was another work that made a deep impression on the young writer.

From New York to Paris

During Hughes's last years of high school, James Hughes re-entered his life. A wealthy mining businessman down in Mexico, he convinced his son to spend the summer of 1919 living with him at his estate in Toluca, Mexico. After Hughes graduated from high school in 1920, he returned to Mexico again, teaching English to Mexican schoolchildren and attempting to make an emotional connection with his father. James Hughes, though, was a demanding and humorless man who was contemptuous of impoverished blacks and Hispanics, and the father and son never became close.

In 1921 Hughes returned to America and enrolled at Columbia University in New York City. His father had agreed to pay his tuition, provided he studied mining engineering. After two semesters, though, Hughes abandoned Columbia in favor of a life of poetry and adventure.

By the time Hughes walked away from Columbia, he was already a published poet. His poem "The Negro Speaks of Rivers" had been published in 1921 in *The Crisis,* the literary magazine of the National Association for the Advancement of Colored People (NAACP). Years later, Hughes still described this early poem as one of the finest of his legendary career—an assessment with which many critics agree. The poem, which celebrated the historic importance of people of African descent and celebrated their grace and spirit, announced that a major new American literary talent was on the horizon.

Several other Hughes poems appeared in the early 1920s in the pages of *The Crisis,* which was guided by Du Bois and Jessie Redmon Fauset. But Hughes's impact on the early Harlem Renaissance was limited by the fact that he spent little time in Harlem—or even in the United States. Instead, the young poet's desire to see the world led him to spend much of 1923 as a crew member on a steamer that crossed the Atlantic and traveled up and down the western coast of Africa. A year later he worked on another steamer, this one bound for Europe. Once in Europe, Hughes left the ship and spent months wandering the streets and cafes of Paris, France. During his time in the so-called "City of Light," Hughes reveled in the performances of African-American blues and jazz singers who had moved to Europe to escape the racism and discrimination that plagued America.

The "Busboy Poet" Becomes a Renaissance Star

Hughes returned to the United States in late 1924. He divided his time between Washington, D.C., where his mother had relocated, and Harlem, the New York City neighborhood that had become the center of the emerging cultural celebration known as the Harlem Renaissance.

Over the next two years Hughes led a strange existence. He spent a lot of time working as a hotel porter, restaurant busboy, and in other low-paying jobs to keep a modest roof over his head. In Harlem, though, he quickly became the most beloved and popular poet of the Renaissance. Poems such as "The Weary Blues," "Mother to Son," "My People," "Danse Africaine" and many others were hailed for their beauty and for their power to capture black feelings, music, and outlooks. Influential black intellectuals and activists such as Du Bois, Alain Locke, and James Weldon Johnson sang his praises, and other respected writers like Countee Cullen and Zora Neale Hurston became close friends. By the end of 1926, black newspapers in New York City and other northern cities were referring to Hughes as the "busboy poet."

By the end of 1927 Hughes had also published two poetry collections, the critically acclaimed *The Weary Blues* (1926) and *Fine Clothes to the Jew* (1927). These books further cemented Hughes's emerging status as the "poet laureate" of the Renaissance (although some black reviewers worried that *Fine Clothes to the Jew* provided too many negative images of blacks). Charles S. Johnson, editor of the National Urban League literary magazine *Opportunity*, explained Hughes's popularity and impact: "No Negro writer so completely symbolizes the new emancipation of the Negro mind. His was a poetry of gorgeous colors, of restless brooding, of melancholy, of disillusionment. . . . Hughes gave a warm glow of meaning to their lives."

A Question of Artistic Independence

Hughes was reaching the peak of his Renaissance influence when he boldly added his perspective to a growing area of debate within the movement. Dating back to the very beginning of the Harlem Renaissance, leading African-American intellectuals and civil rights activists had seen uplifting and positive portrayals of black life and culture as a weapon that could help end racial segregation and discrimination in American society. But many of the movement's young writers and artists felt that Harlem's gritty blues clubs and working-class streets also deserved to be examined and celebrated, and they argued that efforts to control the content of their works posed a threat to their artistic integrity.

In 1926 Hughes published an essay called "The Negro Artist and the Racial Mountain" in *The Nation* that left no doubt where he stood on this issue. He declared his intention to pursue a course of artistic independence and explore all facets of African-American life. Hughes also asserted that the younger writers and artists of the Renaissance did not care whether their work was embraced by black *or* white readers. "We will build our temples for tomorrow, strong as we know how, and we will stand on top of the mountain, free within ourselves," he stated.

Over the next few years Hughes made good on his promise. He was a key member of the Harlem group that published the radical *Fire!!* literary magazine, which was condemned by W.E.B. Du Bois and other conservative black voices. In addition, many of Hughes's own poems used the language and setting of Harlem's streets and speakeasies. But the humanity of the prostitutes, drinkers, laborers, and blues singers that walked through his poems always shone through.

In the late 1920s, though, Hughes's determination to maintain complete artistic independence also was strongly tested. In 1927 he was introduced to Charlotte Osgood Mason, a wealthy white supporter of the Harlem Renaissance. The generous assistance of Mason—known to Hughes and other beneficiaries as "Mother"—enabled Hughes to quit working and devote all his energies to writing. By the end of the decade, though, Hughes had grown uncomfortable with Mason's efforts to shape the direction of his work and life. He tried to end their relationship gently, but Mason was so angered that she cut off all ties to the poet.

After the Renaissance

Although his relationship with Mason ended unhappily, Hughes enjoyed many personal triumphs in the late 1920s and early 1930s. In 1929 he earned a bachelor's degree from Lincoln University in Pennsylvania. One year later, his first novel, *Not Without Laughter,* won the Harmon Gold Medal for literature. He also continued to publish numerous poems, even as many other poets and writers associated with the Harlem Renaissance were falling silent. In 1935 his dramatic play *Mulatto,* which focused on the relationship between a white father and his mulatto son, was unveiled on Broadway to critical and popular acclaim.

Hughes also traveled widely in the 1930s, touring large swaths of the American South as well as the Soviet Union, China, Korea, Japan, and Mexico. In the late 1930s the restless Hughes even went to Spain and reported on the Spanish Civil War for the *Pittsburgh Courier.* During this period Hughes's political beliefs took a sharp turn to the left and he became convinced that socialism was superior to American-style capitalism.

Hughes's work in Spain as a correspondent marked his only foray into reporting. Hughes quickly returned to creative writing. In 1945 he published his autobiography, *The Big Sea,* which included fascinating glimpses into the heyday of the Harlem Renaissance. The success of *Mulatto,* meanwhile, ushered in a period of prolific playwriting for Hughes. He wrote six more plays through the 1940s, and he founded three theater companies—the Harlem Suitcase Theater in New York, the New Negro Theater in Los Angeles, and the Skyloft Players in Chicago. In 1947 he wrote the lyrics for the hit Broadway musical play *Street Scene.* Earnings from *Street Scene* brought Hughes more financial security than he had ever had before, and he promptly bought a townhouse in Harlem.

During this same period Hughes introduced the fictional character of Jesse B. Semple, nicknamed "Simple," to American readers. Simple first appeared in 1943 in the *Chicago Defender,* a leading black newspaper to which Hughes regularly contributed a column. The character of Simple, a poor and luckless—but likable—resident of Harlem, was an immediate hit. Over the next several years, Hughes regularly used the character of Simple to humorously and poignantly comment on the challenges of being a black man in a racist country. The stories were eventually collected in several books, the first of which was the 1950 collection *Simple Speaks His Mind.*

A Rich and Varied Career

Hughes's political beliefs became a growing focus of criticism after the conclusion of World War II. After the war ended in 1945, the United States and the Soviet Union launched a nearly five-decade long political and military rivalry that became known as the Cold War. Fear and hatred of Communism and its supporters soared all across America. By the late 1940s numerous Congressional committees and law enforcement agencies were seeking out Communist "spies" in every corner of American life.

In 1953 Hughes was called to testify before Senator Joe McCarthy's notorious Congressional committee devoted to exposing Communist agents in America. Hughes never identified any of his old friends or colleagues as Communists, but he disowned his left-wing statements and poetry of the 1930s. And unlike some other men and women called to testify, Hughes never challenged the profoundly destructive effects of McCarthy's Communist "witch hunts" on American society in the 1950s. Instead, fear for his career led him to adopt a deferential and cooperative demeanor throughout his testimony.

Once his encounter with McCarthy was over, Hughes resumed his productive literary career. During the 1950s and 1960s he wrote novels, short stories, children's stories, plays, and poetry, including *Montage of a Dream Deferred* (1951), an ambitious book-length poem that traced the history of Harlem in verse. Hughes also joined with Arna Bontemps to edit two important anthologies of African-American culture, *The Poetry of the Negro* (1949) and *The Book of Negro Folklore* (1958).

In all of these works, the warmth and affection that Hughes felt for his fellow African Americans shone through. Writing in the April 1952 issue of the *Saturday Review,* Arna Bontemps speculated that the generous spirit of

Hughes's writing reflected his own strong sense of self-worth. "Few people have enjoyed being Negro as much as Langston Hughes," said Bontemps. "Despite the bitterness with which he has occasionally indicted those who mistreat him because of his color . . . there has never been any question in this reader's mind about his basic attitude. He would not have missed the experience of being what he is for the world."

Hughes died on May 22, 1967, in New York City after an operation for a benign prostate condition. His last book of verse, *The Panther and the Lash,* was published posthumously. Today, Hughes is remembered as one of the most brilliant poets in American history, and as the poet laureate of the Harlem Renaissance era. "Beloved both by fellow writers and ordinary black readers, he stirred and returned that affection in verse that celebrated black life and culture as it had never been celebrated before," wrote biographer Arnold Rampersad in *Harlem Speaks.*

Sources:

Berry, Faith. *Before and Beyond Harlem: A Biography of Langston Hughes.* New York: Random House, 1995.

Hughes, Langston. *The Big Sea: An Autobiography.* New York: Knopf, 1945.

Hughes, Langston. *The Collected Poems of Langston Hughes.* Edited by Arnold Rampersad. New York: Vintage, 1995.

Johnson, Charles S. "The Negro Renaissance and Its Significance." In *The Portable Harlem Renaissance Reader.* Edited by David Levering Lewis. New York: Penguin, 1994.

Miller, R. Baxter. *The Art and Imagination of Langston Hughes.* Lexington: University Press of Kentucky, 2006.

Rampersad, Arnold. *The Life of Langston Hughes. Volume 1: 1902-1942: I, Too, Sing America,* and *Volume II: 1941-1967: I Dream a World.* New York: Oxford University Press, 1986, 1988.

Rampersad, Arnold. "Langston Hughes." In *Harlem Speaks: A Living History of the Harlem Renaissance.* Edited by Cary D. Wintz. Naperville, IL: Sourcebooks, 2007.

Tracy, Steven C. *Langston Hughes and the Blues.* Urbana: University of Illinois Press, 2001.

Zora Neale Hurston (1891-1960)
Novelist and Southern Folklorist

Photographed by Carl Van Vechten.

Historians believe that Zora Neale Lee Hurston was born on January 7, 1891. She was born in Notasulga, Alabama, but raised from infancy in the rural all-black community of Eatonville, Florida. This small city, which was first established in 1887, was the nation's first incorporated black township. Zora's mother was Lucy Ann (Potts) Hurston. Her father was John Hurston, a carpenter and part-time preacher who also served as mayor of Eatonville for several years.

Hurston and her many brothers and sisters enjoyed daily life in rural Eatonville, which, unlike most other Deep South communities, was not shaped by white racism. "In Eatonville," wrote biographer Valerie Boyd, "Zora was never indoctrinated in inferiority, and she could see the evidence of black achievement all around her. She could look to town hall and see black men, including her father, John Hurston, formulating the laws that governed Eatonville. She could look to the Sunday Schools of the town's two churches and see black women, including her mother, Lucy Potts Hurston, directing the Christian curricula. She could look to the porch of the village store and see black men and women passing worlds through their mouths in the form of colorful, engaging stories."

Hurston had a very close and affectionate relationship with her mother, who she later described as an always-encouraging presence in her life. After Lucy Hurston died in 1904, though, her father quickly remarried a woman that Zora despised. Within a matter of months, John Hurston had essentially abandoned Zora, who responded by leaving home. The "hour" of her mother's death "began my wanderings," she later wrote. "Not so much in geography, but in time. Then not so much in time as in spirit."

Travels Lead to New York

Historians know virtually nothing about Hurston's life in the years immediately after her departure from Eatonville. Her experiences during this period—jobs held, romantic relationships, and so on—are a complete mystery. Eventually, however, she reappeared in the historical record. In 1915 she was living in Memphis, Tennessee, with one of her brothers when she secured employment as a maid with a traveling troupe of actors that performed Gilbert and Sullivan comic operas.

By 1917 Hurston had landed in Baltimore, Maryland, where she decided to resume her high school education. In order to qualify for free public schooling, which was only available to teens, she shaved ten years off her age in her application. Fortunately for the 26-year-old Hurston, she had the youthful appearance to pull off the deception. From that point forward, she always claimed that she had been born in 1901.

In 1918 Hurston earned her high school diploma and moved to Washington, D.C., where she supported herself as a maid while attending classes at Howard University, one of the nation's most prestigious black schools. During this time she began writing short stories and poetry. These early efforts deeply impressed Alain Locke, a Howard professor who was also one of America's leading black intellectuals. Locke brought Hurston's work to the attention of Charles S. Johnson, editor of the National Urban League's literary magazine *Opportunity*. From this point forward, Hurston often published her work in *Opportunity*—and Johnson became one of her greatest supporters.

In 1925 Johnson helped Hurston move to New York City, where she supported herself as a personal assistant to the white novelist Fannie Hurst. Within weeks of her arrival, she had taken the city's black intellectual and literary community by storm. Outgoing and exuberant, she was soon regularly attending social gatherings at the homes of many leading figures of the Harlem Renaissance, from Jessie Redmon Fauset to James Weldon Johnson. She also established relationships with liberal white supporters of the Renaissance such as Carl Van Vechten, who became a close friend, and Charlotte Osgood Mason, who emerged as an important patron.

During the next few years, Hurston became well-known for her poetry and short stories, her fascination with African-American folk tales, and her outspoken, energetic personality. She also coined some of the most famous terms to come out of the Renaissance era, including "negrotarian" (wealthy white philanthropists who support black artists) and "niggerati." Hurston and other outspoken black writers used "niggerati"—a combination of "nigger" and "literati"—to refer to both themselves and other intellectuals of the

Harlem Renaissance. Hurston and her friends saw it as a playful term that poked fun at cultural elitism. Other black leaders deeply disapproved of the term because of its racist roots.

Queen of the Renaissance

By the late 1920s, some Harlemites were calling Hurston the "Queen of the Renaissance," a title she laughingly embraced. But others resented her rise because they felt that she was forever skirting the subject of white racism—both in her work and in her personal life. One of her best friends in Harlem, poet Langston Hughes, understood both of these perspectives on Hurston. "In her youth she was always getting scholarships and things from wealthy white people, some of whom simply paid her to just sit around and represent the Negro race for them, she did it in such racy fashion," he wrote in *The Big Sea*. "To many of her white friends, no doubt, she was the perfect 'darkie' in the nice meaning they give the term—that is, naïve, childlike, sweet, humorous and highly-colored Negro. . . . But Miss Hurston was clever, too. . . . and had great scorn for all pretensions, academic or otherwise."

For her part, Hurston dismissed the criticisms of African Americans who thought that she did not pay enough attention to the nation's slaveholding history or its ongoing "race problem." "I am not tragically colored," she declared in a famous 1928 essay she titled "How It Feels To Be Colored Me." "I do not weep at the world—I am too busy sharpening my oyster knife."

In addition to writing, Hurston continued her educational pursuits in New York. She enrolled at Barnard College, where she studied anthropology under the famed anthropologist Franz Boas. She received her bachelor's degree from Barnard in 1927. That same year, she was married. But this marriage, like two others in 1939 and 1944, lasted for less than a year before falling apart.

From Novels to Folktale Collections

Hurston's literary contributions to the Harlem Renaissance during the 1920s were limited to poems, short stories, and a couple of plays. She also was an important contributor in 1926 to the lone issue of the famous literary magazine *Fire!!* spearheaded by Wallace Thurman.

It was in the 1930s, though, that Hurston made her greatest mark on the Renaissance. The decade got off to a rocky start in 1930, when her friendship with Hughes was destroyed by a dispute over authorship of *Mule Bone*, a play that the two had worked on together. Over the subsequent few years, though, Hurston earned several important scholarships—including a Rosenwald Fellowship in 1934 and Guggenheim fellowships in 1936 and 1937—that gave her the financial independence to write her greatest works.

The first of these works was *Jonah's Gourd Vine*, a 1934 novel loosely based on Hurston's own childhood memories of life in Eatonville. As in many of her other stories and poems, the author relied on "black dialect" or "black speech" as a narrative device in the novel. (Hurston's use of black country dialect in her novels, stories, and folk tale collections—complete with odd spellings, nontraditional grammar, and other syntax not adjusted for formal written text—has been criticized by some for perpetuating racial stereotypes, but praised by others for authenticity and historical accuracy.)

In 1935 Hurston published *Mules and Men*, a vibrant collection of black folk tales gathered during extended travels through the Deep South in the early 1930s. This work continues to rank as a milestone in the historical preservation of traditional African-American folklore. A second collection of folk tales gathered from Jamaica and Haiti, called *Tell My Horse*, was released by Hurston in 1938.

Another of Hurston's major triumphs was *Their Eyes Were Watching God*, a 1937 novel that many critics cite as her masterpiece. The story, which follows a middle-aged black woman as she navigates the racial and sexual politics of an oppressive society, has been hailed by some scholars as an early example of black feminism in American literature. "It remains one of the great novels of black literature," wrote scholar Jennifer Jordan. "A novel that is laughing out-loud funny, that allows black people to speak in their own wonderful voices, and that portrays them in all their human nobility and pettiness."

Hurston's next book was the 1939 novel *Moses, Man of the Mountain*, which retold the story of the Biblical Moses through the prism of African-American folklore and history. Her last major work was *Dust Tracks on a Road*, her 1942 autobiography. In this memoir, Hurston once again defended herself from critics who had ripped her over the years for avoiding America's brutal history of racial subjugation and discrimination. "While I have a handkerchief over my eyes crying over the landing of the first slaves in 1619, I might miss something swell that is going on in 1942," she wrote.

Scandal and Obscurity

Hurston roamed constantly during the 1930s and 1940s, spending extended periods of time in Latin America, Florida, North Carolina, New York, and even California, where she worked as consultant for Paramount Pictures. By the mid-1940s, however, the Harlem Renaissance was only a memory and publishers were no longer interested in her work. As her literary career faded, Hurston experienced growing financial problems.

Hurston's life took another grim turn in 1948, when she was accused of molesting a young boy in New York City. The accusation was treated as a major scandal in the black press. Hurston was innocent, and the charges were eventually dropped. But the legal fees that she had to pay to defend herself took an additional toll on her shaky financial situation, and the whole incident left her with deep emotional scars.

In 1950 Hurston moved to Florida, where she worked as a librarian, maid, and teacher. She continued her fade into obscurity over the remainder of the decade. The only time that she returned to the spotlight was in 1955, when she wrote a controversial letter to the editor of the *Orlando Sentinel* about efforts to desegregate America's schools. The letter was widely interpreted in the black community as a defense of segregation, and it triggered a wave of condemnation from African-American civil rights leaders.

In 1959 Hurston suffered a stroke that forced her to move into a welfare home. She died on January 28, 1960, and was buried in an unmarked grave in a segregated cemetery in St. Lucie County, Florida. In 1973 the noted African-American novelist Alice Walker made a pilgrimage to the gravesite of Hurston, who Walker has long cited as a major literary influence. When she saw that Hurston's grave was unmarked, Walker paid for a headstone. The marker, which remains there today, reads: "Zora Neale Hurston, A Genius of the South."

When Hurston died she was an impoverished and forgotten woman. But Walker and other leading African-American writers have cited her novels as major inspirations for their own careers, and today Hurston's work is read and studied in schools and universities across the nation.

Sources:
Boyd, Valerie: *Wrapped in Rainbows: The Life of Zora Neale Hurston.* New York: Scribner, 2003.
Hemenway, Robert. "Zora Neale Hurston and the Eatonville Anthropology," in *The Harlem Renaissance Remembered.* Edited by Arna Bontemps. New York: Dodd, Mead, 1972.

Hurston, Zora Neale. *Dust Tracks on a Road.* Foreword by Maya Angelou. New York: Harper Perennial, 1991.

Jordan, Jennifer. "Feminist Fantasies: Zora Neale Hurston's *Their Eyes Were Watching God,*" *Tulsa Studies in Women's Literature,* vol. 7, no. 1, Spring 1988.

Walker, Alice. "In Search of Zora Neale Hurston." *Ms Magazine,* March 1975.

Zora Neale Hurston website. Available online at *zoranealehurston.com.* Accessed September 2007.

James Weldon Johnson (1871-1938)

Author, Journalist, Lyricist, and Diplomat Who Served as Executive Secretary of the NAACP During the Renaissance Era

James William Johnson was born in Jacksonville, Florida, on June 17, 1871. He changed his middle name to "Weldon" in 1913. His father, James Johnson, was headwaiter at a luxury hotel. His mother, Helen, was a schoolteacher from the Bahamas. Compared to most African Americans of the era, both of his parents were well-educated and financially comfortable. They were thus able to provide a nurturing and positive home environment for James and his younger brother John Rosamond, who was born in 1873. Both parents instilled in their sons a love for music and literature at an early age, and they were able to insulate the boys from the worst of the racism that saturated the Deep South in the post-Reconstruction era.

After completing his elementary schooling, Johnson confronted the first major discriminatory hurdle of his young life. Black youths in Jacksonville were excluded from the city's high schools, but he wanted to continue his education. His parents supported his ambitions, so they enrolled him at Georgia's Atlanta University, a black college that also maintained a secondary school. He spent the next several years excelling in his studies, and he earned his bachelor's degree from the school in 1894.

Johnson also learned a lot outside the classroom during his years in Atlanta. During his last few years at the school, he spent his summer breaks teaching black children in remote corners of Georgia. This extended exposure to impoverished, disillusioned, and frightened black families living under the shadow of Jim Crow laws made an enormous impression on him. Johnson also witnessed several depressing examples of racial discrimination and white hatred during his travels through the South as a member of a school-affiliated singing group called the Atlanta University Quartet.

Renaissance Man

After leaving Atlanta University with his diploma in hand, Johnson embarked on a restless and ambitious path that made him a "Renaissance man"—educated and talented in numerous areas—years before the Harlem Renaissance even came into existence.

The first step in Johnson's development into what scholar David Levering Lewis termed "a suave, self-created success on a heroic scale" was to accept a position as principal of Stanton Public School in Jacksonville in 1894. Within a few years, Johnson had expanded the elementary school's curriculum so that it could provide a secondary education to the city's black youth. Stanton thus became the first public high school for African Americans in Florida history.

Johnson remained principal at Stanton until 1902, but he also pursued many other interests during the mid and late 1890s. In 1895 he founded the *Daily American,* the first daily newspaper in the history of the United States to be aimed at an African-American audience (it was not financially successful, so it folded after eight months). Johnson also continued his education during these years, studying music and law. In 1897 he became the first African-American lawyer ever to gain admittance to the Florida Bar Association, and he earned a master's degree in music from Atlanta University in 1904.

Johnson's enormously long and successful career as a lyricist also began during this period. In 1899 his brother Rosamond returned to Jacksonville after an extended stay in New York City. The younger Johnson brother had already begun a career in musical show business, and he convinced his elder brother to collaborate with him on songs and musicals. One of the songs they wrote and put to music over the next year was "Lift Every Voice and Sing," a song of patriotism and hoped-for racial "liberty." Nineteen years later, this popular song was adopted by the NAACP as the "Negro National Anthem," and it became a beloved fixture in black churches and other social gatherings across America.

To New York City

In 1902 the Johnson brothers moved to New York City to pursue careers in musical theater. They quickly established a strong working relationship with black composer Bob Cole, a rising star on the black vaudeville circuit. Over the next several years, Cole and the Johnson brothers collaborated on more than 200 songs for the musical theater. Many of these songs, such as

"Oh Didn't He Ramble" and "Under the Bamboo Tree," brought a new level of sophistication to the black stage, and they were performed by some of the leading singers of the era. In addition, the trio wrote and composed a popular musical comedy for the stage called *The Shoo-Fly Regiment* (1906).

By 1905 Cole and Rosemond Johnson had also developed a popular vaudeville act. Their show was so successful that they were offered extended bookings at theaters in London, England, and Paris, France. They seized the opportunity, and James went along as their road manager. During this time in Europe, James was able to explore London, Paris, Amsterdam, and other great cities. Like New York City, the streets of these cities were cosmopolitan and hummed with energy. But unlike New York and other large American cities, they were virtually free of racism. Johnson savored every moment of his time in Europe.

When Cole and the Johnson brothers returned to the United States, Cole and Rosamond resumed their vaudeville touring and James moved on to other interests. He took classes at Columbia University and became a leading figure in the Colored Republicans Club, which supported the presidential campaign of Theodore Roosevelt. Johnson also became known as a supporter of Booker T. Washington and his philosophy of racial harmony, which emphasized black economic self-sufficiency over equal civil rights.

A Diplomatic Career in Latin America

In 1906 President Roosevelt rewarded Johnson for his support by appointing him to the post of U.S. consul in Puerto Cabello, Venezuela. Johnson's duties were light, so he was able to spend a lot of time pursuing his interest in poetry. Several of these poems were published in America over the next few years. The best-known of these poems was "O Black and Unknown Bards," a tribute to the men and women who gave voice to traditional black spirituals. In addition, Johnson began work on his novel *The Autobiography of an Ex-Colored Man* during this time.

Johnson remained in Venezuela for three years before receiving a transfer to a diplomatic post in Nicaragua. He arrived in Nicaragua at a time of great political turmoil, as a popular revolt threatened the stability of the country's pro-American government. At one point Johnson actually supervised the defense of the port city of Corinto against a looming rebel attack until U.S. Marines arrived. He also left bachelorhood behind during his time in Nicaragua. In 1910 he married Grace Nail, a member of one of Harlem's wealthiest black families.

In January 1913 Woodrow Wilson was inaugurated as the 28th president of the United States. The Wilson administration wasted little time in removing black workers from the federal payroll and imposing segregationist rules and regulations in federal agencies. Johnson's diplomatic career was one of the casualties of this swift and demoralizing setback for black civil rights.

From Novelist to Civil Rights Activist

Only a few months before Johnson's career as a diplomat was snuffed out, his novel *The Autobiography of an Ex-Colored Man* was published in the United States. But the novel—the only one that Johnson ever wrote—was published anonymously because of a belief that it would be shunned if it was known that a black man had written it. The book traces the life of a light-skinned black man who decides to "pass" for white when he witnesses a horrifying lynching of a black man. He abandons his musical gifts in favor of a career in real estate, begins a family with a white woman, and even seems to embrace some white racist attitudes. But at the end of the novel the widowed protagonist looks back on his decision to forsake his black heritage with regret. "I have sold my birthright for a mess of pottage," he declares in the last sentence of the book.

Since *The Autobiography of an Ex-Colored Man* was published anonymously, it did not advance Johnson's career. But Washington cushioned his dismissal from government service by helping him get a job as an editorial writer for the *New York Age,* the oldest African-American newspaper in the city. Johnson's editorials reflected his fierce desire to break the patterns of racism and discrimination that had a stranglehold on the nation. Over time, they also showed Johnson's gradual move away from Washington's political philosophy and toward the views championed by W.E.B. Du Bois and other leading voices for integration and equal rights. Johnson wrote for the *Age* until 1923.

Johnson's evolving political views became even more evident in 1916, when he accepted an offer to become field secretary for the National Association for the Advancement of Colored People (NAACP). The job, for which he was actively recruited by Du Bois and Joel Springarn, the white president of the organization, called for him to organize NAACP membership drives, civil rights demonstrations, and other activities all across the country.

Johnson proved to be an excellent choice. He spearheaded a fantastically successful membership drive that greatly increased the size and influence of the NAACP. In addition, he planned a number of effective demonstrations and campaigns against white discrimination and violence. For example, Johnson took a lead role in organizing the famous 1917 Silent March of black men, women, and children through the heart of New York City to protest lynchings and other acts of terrorism by whites. "The streets of New York witnessed many strange sights but, I judge, never one more impressive," Johnson later recalled. "The parade moved in silence and was watched in silence." He also was instrumental in the passage of the Dyer Anti-Lynching Bill two years later.

Chronicler of Black Poetry and Spirituals

In 1920 Johnson was named executive secretary of the NAACP, succeeding Springarn. His ongoing work for the NAACP made him one of the recognized leaders of the "New Negro Movement" that was dedicated to ending segregation and racism in America. These efforts were given additional momentum by the Harlem Renaissance, the exciting African-American literary and artistic movement that flowered in New York City in the early 1920s.

Over the next several years, Johnson himself made important contributions to the literature of the Harlem Renaissance. In 1922 he edited *The Book of American Negro Poetry,* a collection that shone a spotlight on the work of the nation's talented but long-neglected black poets. In his foreword to this volume, Johnson boldly stated his belief that African-American literature and art had the capacity to bash down America's racist walls by demonstrating black capabilities and presenting positive images of black people and culture. Johnson would repeat this belief over and over again for the remainder of the 1920s.

In 1925 Johnson collaborated with his brother Rosamond to publish two major historical collections of traditional Negro spirituals. Two years later, *The Autobiography of an Ex-Colored Man* was republished to wide acclaim—and this time Johnson was listed as the author. In addition, Johnson published essays and poetry in leading black magazines like *The Crisis* and *Opportunity* as well as periodicals with a large white readership, such as *American Mercury* and *Harper's.*

Johnson's most celebrated literary work of the Renaissance era, though, was *God's Trombones: Seven Negro Sermons in Verse.* Written in the language of the rural South, the book set seven powerful traditional sermons to verse. In

131

creating this work, the agnostic Johnson paid tribute to the many black ministers who were pillars of their communities while at the same time embracing African-American folk traditions. The book also featured beautiful illustrations by Aaron Douglas, one of the best-known African-American artists of the Harlem Renaissance. In 1930 he published *Black Manhattan,* a vivid historical account of Harlem's development into the black capital of America.

A Sponsor and Mentor

In addition to his own literary work, Johnson provided important assistance to other poets and novelists of the Harlem Renaissance. He served as a sponsor and mentor to numerous black writers, helping them improve their work, publicize it, and get it published. His close friendships with powerful white members of the New York publishing world, such as writer Carl Van Vechten and publisher Alfred Knopf, gave him the opportunity to advance the careers of many deserving young writers. He was also instrumental in convincing the Julius Rosenwald Fund to extend their fellowships to African-American writers and artists. "He was a man of great culture," recalled Douglas, "and one that was quite capable of inspiring younger men to . . . attempt to do something *worthy* of the opportunities [they received] and worthy of those who had gone before them."

Unlike Du Bois and many other older members of the Talented Tenth, Johnson also respected and understood the perspective of the young rebels of the Harlem Renaissance. When Langston Hughes, Wallace Thurman, and other talented writers asserted that they were going to pursue their artistic visions without worrying about the political fallout, Johnson did not join Du Bois and others who attacked them as betrayers of the civil rights cause. Instead, Johnson optimistically asserted that the quality of the poetry, short stories, novels, and artwork that these men and women created could convince the white world of black equality.

Taking Leave of Harlem

In 1930 Johnson resigned his post at the NAACP, though he was elected to the organization's board of directors. One year later, he left Harlem for a faculty position at Fisk University in Nashville. Johnson left New York City with mixed feelings. He recognized that the crusade for racial equality in America still had a long ways to go, but he also sensed that the Harlem Renaissance was fading in importance and vitality.

Johnson spent the next several years teaching and writing. In 1933 he published his autobiography, *Along This Way*. One year later he published *Negro Americans, What Now?*, in which he urged his fellow African Americans to continue their struggle for integration and equality.

Johnson died on the night of June 26, 1938, in Wiscasset, Maine, when an automobile in which he was riding during a heavy storm was hit by a train at a crossing. His funeral, which was held in New York City, drew an estimated 2,000 mourners. People who came to pay their respects included many giants of the Harlem Renaissance as well as leading city officials such as New York Mayor Fiorello La Guardia. In his eulogy, La Guardia spoke for all those gathered when he declared that Johnson's life was proof that "greatness in a man is a quality that does not know the boundaries of race or creed."

Sources:

Carroll, Anne E. "James Weldon Johnson," in *Harlem Speak.*, Edited by Cary D. Wintz. Naperville, IL: Sourcebooks, 2007.

Fleming, Robert E. *James Weldon Johnson*. Boston: Twayne Publishers, 1987.

Johnson, James Weldon. *James Weldon Johnson: Writings.* Edited by William J. Andrews. New York: Library of America, 2004.

Johnson, James Weldon. *Along This Way: The Autobiography of James Weldon Johnson.* New York: Da Capo Press, 2000.

Nella Larsen (1891-1964)
Renaissance-Era Author of the Novels
Quicksand *and* Passing

Nella Marie Larsen was born Nella Walker on April 13, 1891, in Chicago, Illinois. Her father, who was of West Indian descent, either died or abandoned the family before Nella reached two years of age. Her mother, Mary, was a white Danish woman who married another Danish immigrant, Peter Larsen, two years later. They quickly had a daughter, Anna Elizabeth.

Nella Larsen spent her first few years in one of Chicago's most impoverished and vice-ridden neighborhoods. In 1895 Mary Larsen took her daughters to Denmark to see relatives—and to escape the grim environment in Chicago. They ended up staying for almost three years before returning to the United States. They settled in a house that Peter Larsen had purchased in their absence, located in a neighborhood dominated by German and Scandinavian immigrant families.

Nella's next several years were very difficult ones for her. Her parents and half-sister were white, but she was clearly a "mulatto"—a person with one white and one black parent. Her appearance made life more difficult for the entire family, especially in the early 1900s, when rising levels of bigotry and racial intolerance swept through Chicago and many other northern cities. By the time she entered seventh grade, her parents had enrolled her and her younger sister in separate schools. This scheme was meant to protect Anna from harassment and accusations that she too was black. But it was also an indication that Nella's parents were willing to sacrifice her happiness to make their lives easier.

Abandoned by Family

In 1907 Larsen's parents enrolled her in all-black Fisk University's high school program. A short time later, they cut off all ties with their mulatto daughter, who they viewed as an embarrassment and an obstacle to the pursuit of their own hopes and dreams. Larsen was profoundly shaken by this development. Her self-esteem suffered another terrible blow at the end of the year, when school officials told her not to return. This rejection was punishment for Larsen's participation in student protests against some of the school's many rules regarding dress and decorum.

Wounded and angry, Larsen retreated to Denmark, living with relatives in Copenhagen from 1908 to 1912. During this time she immersed herself in European literature of the era, much of which focused on the moral failures of the middle-class and the social, political, and sexual repression of women.

Larsen returned to the United States in 1912 and began studying nursing at Lincoln Hospital in New York City. After earning her degree in 1915, she accepted an offer to work as a head nurse at Booker T. Washington Tuskegee Institute in Alabama. The institute included both a hospital and a nurse training school on the grounds, so Larsen was kept busy. She soon developed an intense dislike for the Institute, however. She felt that the administrators and faculty treated the students poorly—and that they in essence were teaching them to accept their inferior status in American society.

Larsen abruptly resigned from her position at Tuskegee and returned to New York, taking a nursing job at Lincoln Hospital. In 1918 she joined the city's Bureau of Preventable Diseases. This job took her into various city neighborhoods, where she taught hygiene, sanitation, and other aspects of health education to immigrant families. This position put Larsen on the front lines of the city's response to the deadly Spanish flu epidemic of 1918-19. This epidemic claimed the lives of more than 675,000 Americans from September 1918 through June 1919. But even though New York City suffered more flu cases than any other American city, its death rate was far lower, mostly because of the tireless efforts of Larsen and the other members of the bureau.

Making a Life in Harlem

In May 1919 Larsen married Dr. Elmer S. Imes, a physicist and member of the Fisk University faculty who moved in the same social circles as W.E.B. Du Bois, James Weldon Johnson, and other members of the so-called "Talented Tenth"—educated and cultured African Americans who recognized their obligation to push for social change on behalf of all black Americans. Larsen and her husband settled in Jersey City, on the west bank of the Hudson River directly across from New York City's Manhattan Island.

Over the next few years, Larsen's life underwent enormous changes. Inspired by the example of other young black writers who were producing exciting work from their base in Harlem, Larsen began exploring a writing career as well. In 1920 she published two articles on Danish games and riddles for *The Brownies' Book,* a children's magazine produced by the National Association for the Advancement of Colored People (NAACP). She used the pen name "Allen Semi" (Nella Imes in reverse) for these articles, as well as several short stories that she published in the mid-1920s.

In 1921 Larsen left her nursing career behind and became a librarian in the New York Public Library system. After a brief stint at the Seward Park branch, she gained a transfer to the children's department of the famed Harlem branch on 135th Street. The Harlem library was a favorite meeting place for the early movers and shakers of the Harlem Renaissance, and Larsen enjoyed the high spirits and intellectual vigor of these gatherings.

Larsen made several close friends among New York's literary and intellectual elite during the early and mid-1920s. These friends ranged from controversial figures such as white novelist Carl Van Vechten, author of *Nigger Heaven,* to widely respected figures like *Opportunity* editor Charles S. Johnson. But she made fewer friends in New York's black professional community, which was wary of her independent and opinionated personality and her unconventional ways. Her enjoyment of cigarettes and her disdain for organized religion, for example, were quite unusual for middle-class women of that era.

Exploring America's Color Line

Larsen began working on her first novel, *Quicksand,* in 1926. It was published two years later by publisher Alfred E. Knopf, a leading supporter of black writers of the Harlem Renaissance. *Quicksand* told the story of Helga Crane, a mulatto rejected by both white and black society. Larsen's decision to explore the subject of mixed-race Americans was a potentially explosive one, as some members of the black community viewed African-American discrimination based on skin color as a taboo subject. *Quicksand*'s harsh portrayals of the black middle-class, male attitudes toward female sexuality, and the Tuskegee Institute also were risky. But the novel won praise from influential black leaders, and Larsen was awarded the Harmon Foundation bronze medal for literature in 1928

One year later, Larsen's second novel examining the "color line" in American society was published. The central character in *Passing* was Clare Kendry, a mixed-race woman who is able to "pass" for white. She even marries a white man who is an avowed racist. The deceptions of this life eventually lead Clare to try to reconnect with the black world she left behind, with tragic results. Writing in *The Crisis*, Du Bois expressed admiration for Larsen's efforts to shine a light on the lives of mulatto Americans in a racist society. "It is a difficult task, but she attacks the problem fearlessly and with consummate art," he wrote.

After *Passing* was published, Larsen received a Guggenheim Fellowship to help her write a third novel. Around the same time, though, she was accused of plagiarism in a short story, "Sanctuary," that was published in *Forum*, a prestigious magazine of the Jazz Age era. The charges were false, but the controversy shook Larsen's faith about her place in the Harlem Renaissance movement.

In 1930 Larsen traveled to Europe to conduct research for her next novel, but her travels were ruined by the discovery that her husband was carrying on an affair with a white woman at Fisk. When she returned to the United States after sixteen months in Europe, she reluctantly rejoined her husband at Fisk. By this time, however, the emotional ties between them had been destroyed. In addition, Larsen sensed that many faculty and students at Fisk viewed her as an outsider and troublemaker.

These events pushed Larsen into a period of self-destructive behavior that included two half-hearted suicide attempts. Finally she sued for divorce, ending her marriage to Imes after fourteen years. She then moved back to New York City, where she worked as a nurse for the next thirty years. Larsen completely abandoned her writing career after returning to New York, and she cut all of her social ties with her old Harlem friends. She reportedly struggled with alcoholism and drug abuse at various periods of her later life, and a few attempts she made to reconcile with white family members were rejected.

Larsen was forced to retire from nursing in 1963, when hospital administrators discovered that she was past the retirement age of seventy. She died eight months later of a heart attack, on March 30, 1964. When her sister and other white relatives were informed of her death, they denied having any previous knowledge of her existence.

Larsen's life was in many ways a tragic one, marked by rejection and struggle. The two books she wrote during the height of the Harlem Renaissance, though, are regarded by many scholars as among the finest novels of the entire movement. As George Hutchinson wrote in *Harlem Speaks*, "they remain unmatched as explorations of the psychology of the color-line and the high cost of resisting it."

Sources:

Bloom, Harold, ed. *Black American Prose Writers of the Harlem Renaissance.* New York: Chelsea House, 1994.

Davis, Thadious M. *Nella Larsen, Novelist of the Harlem Renaissance: A Woman's Life Unveiled.* Baton Rouge: Louisiana State University Press, 1994.

Hutchinson, George. *In Search of Nella Larsen: A Biography of the Color Line.* Cambridge, MA: Belknap Press of Harvard University Press, 2006.

Hutchinson, George. "Nella Larsen." In *Harlem Speaks.* Edited by Cary D. Wintz. Naperville, IL: Sourcebooks, 2007.

Alain Locke (1885-1954)
Scholar, Editor, and Supporter of the Harlem Renaissance

Alain Leroy Locke was born on September 13, 1885, in Philadelphia, Pennsylvania. He was the only child of Pliny Ishmael Locke, who worked with the Reconstruction-era Freedmen's Bureau before moving on to a job with the U.S. Post Office, and Mary Hawkins, who was a teacher.

Locke contracted rheumatic fever as a child, and the disease permanently limited his ability to participate in physical activities. He also lost his father when he was only six years old. But his mother was able to support them both on her teacher's salary, and she cultivated in her son a deep love for books and music. By his teen years he could play both the piano and the violin, and he was an enthusiastic reader of classic literature.

After graduating from high school in 1902, Locke entered Harvard University. He completed the school's four-year bachelor's degree program in three years and graduated with honors in 1907. He also received the school's most prestigious award, the Bowdoin Prize. In 1907 Locke became the first African American in U.S. history to receive a Rhodes Scholarship, a prestigious fellowship to study at Oxford University in England.

Locke studied at Oxford until 1910 and then moved on to study philosophy at the University of Berlin. He returned to the United States early in 1912. Despite his many accomplishments and impressive academic training, faculty positions at most American colleges and universities were closed to him because of his skin color. He took a six-month tour of the American South, where his worst fears about the plight of southern blacks were confirmed, then accepted a teaching position at Howard University, a college for African Americans in Washington, D.C.

From Howard to Harlem

Locke became a major figure at Howard during the 1910s. He was one of the school's most respected teachers, and his efforts to establish the school as a center for the study of African-American culture and history were welcomed by many students and instructors. But the school's white president and white board of trustees blocked many of his initiatives, and by the end of the decade relations between Locke and the school administration were strained.

In the meantime, Locke's restless mind and his interest in African-American culture led him to pursue other challenges. In 1916 he resumed his studies at Harvard, taking a leave of absence from Howard. Two years later he earned his doctorate degree in philosophy from the school. Armed with this degree, he was able to secure the chairmanship of the philosophy department at Howard upon his return to the university in 1918.

Locke was also fascinated by events in Harlem during the late 1910s and early 1920s. During this period the Manhattan neighborhood had become a fabled destination for blacks all across America, and it was quickly emerging as a gathering place for talented young African-American novelists, poets, composers, and artists. "Negro life is not only establishing new contacts and founding new centers, it is also finding a new soul [in Harlem]," he wrote in the mid-1920s. "Each group has come with its own separate motives and for its own special ends, but their greatest experience has been the finding of one another."

Locke's reputation as a talented scholar and philosopher grew during the early 1920s, and many of Harlem's leading intellectuals were acquainted with him and his work. But he did not really make his mark on the Harlem Renaissance until 1925, when Locke and several other professors were dismissed from Howard. The administration claimed that the firings were aimed at improving the university's finances and operating efficiency. Many observers, though, asserted that Locke had been dismissed because of his ongoing efforts to shape the curriculum towards African-American studies. Black newspapers ran editorials condemning the school's white administration, and students organized protests against the dismissals. "If such a man of ripe scholarship as that of Dr. Locke cannot teach at Howard University," claimed one statement of protest, "the administration cannot be endeavoring to run Howard as an institution of learning."

Locke's exile from Howard University lasted for three years. He was reinstated to the faculty in 1928 when Mordecai Johnson became the school's first black president. Locke's years away from Howard, though, were enormously beneficial, both to him and to numerous writers of the Harlem Renaissance.

"Mid-Wife" to the Harlem Renaissance

In 1924 Paul Kellogg, the editor of a popular monthly magazine called *Survey Graphic*, approached Locke about serving as guest editor of a special edition of the magazine that would be devoted to Harlem and the cultural movement swirling around it. Locke, who was on sabbatical from Howard at the time, enthusiastically accepted the offer. Several months later, in March 1925, the special issue hit newsstands.

The March 1925 issue of *Survey Graphic*, subtitled *Harlem: Mecca of the New Negro,* created a huge sensation. Locke had seamlessly blended poetry from leading Renaissance writers like Langston Hughes, Claude McKay, and Countee Cullen with essays by black intellectuals such as Walter F. White, James Weldon Johnson, and Charles S. Johnson. Short stories, photographs, and illustrations documenting various aspects of Harlem life also were featured. The final product was a provocative, exciting, and informative snapshot of the Harlem Renaissance of the mid-1920s. Several months later, Locke republished the contents of the special issue—with additional poetry, fiction, drama, and critical essays—in a book anthology titled *The New Negro: An Interpretation.*

From this point forward, Locke became a tireless—and effective—advocate for many of the finest young writers of the Harlem Renaissance, including Cullen, McKay, Zora Neale Hurston, and Langston Hughes. He also advanced the careers of artists like Aaron Douglas. Scholars have speculated that, in at least some cases, Locke's homosexuality may have factored into his interest in their careers. But he was also genuinely devoted to helping deserving young writers and artists, and he was convinced that African-American literature, music, and art could greatly enrich America's cultural heritage and vitality. His role in the Harlem Renaissance, Locke once wrote, was to act as a "philosophical mid-wife to a generation of younger Negro poets, writers, and artists."

One of the most notable ways in which Locke advanced the cause of Renaissance writers and artists was by acquainting them with white publishers, editors, and patrons who were interested in their work. He built a particularly close relationship with Charlotte Osgood Mason, a wealthy white woman who was one of the most influential and generous patrons of the entire Renaissance era. Mason looked to Locke for guidance about which artists she should support, and he was happy to oblige.

After the Renaissance

Locke's role as one of the primary architects of the Harlem Renaissance lasted until the early 1930s. The movement lost much of its vitality at that time. Locke's relationships with Hughes, Hurston, and other leading writers cooled around this period as well. In 1931 he wrote in a letter to Mason that "I hear almost no news from New York; a younger crowd of 'Newer negroes' are dancing in the candle flame. The older ones are nursing their singed wings."

Long after the Renaissance faded away, though, Locke remained deeply interested in African-American literature and art. He remained an internationally recognized expert on African-American culture, and in 1945 he became the first African-American president of the American Association for Adult Education, which was a predominantly white organization. In 1953 he retired from Howard University, which responded by awarding him an honorary doctorate. He moved to New York City, but health problems kept him from enjoying his retirement. Locke died of heart disease in New York on June 9, 1954.

Sources:

Linnemann, Russell J., ed. *Alain Locke: Reflections on a Modern Renaissance Man.* Baton Rouge: Louisiana State University Press, 1982.

Locke, Alain, ed. *The New Negro: An Interpretation.* New York: Albert and Charles Boni, 1925.

Stewart, Jeffrey C. *The Critical Temper of Alain Locke: A Selection of His Essays on Art and Culture.* New York: Garland, 1983.

Paul Robeson (1898-1976)
Actor, Singer, Cultural Scholar, and
Political Activist

Paul Robeson was born in Princeton, New Jersey, on April 9, 1898. His father, William Drew Robeson, had been born into slavery on a North Carolina plantation, but had escaped north at age fifteen on the Underground Railroad. He later became a minister in the Presbyterian and African Methodist Episcopal (AME) Zion churches. Paul Robeson's mother, Maria Louisa Bustill, was a schoolteacher who hailed from a distinguished Philadelphia family.

Paul Robeson's mother died when he was six years old, and a few years later his father moved his nine children to Somerville, New Jersey. During the next several years, his father remained young Paul's primary role model. "Loyalty to one's convictions was the text of my father's life," he later wrote. His father's worship services also exposed Paul to the traditional African-American gospel songs that, years later, would become the foundation of his spectacularly successful singing career.

A Star in the Classroom and on the Sporting Field

At age seventeen Robeson earned an academic scholarship to Rutgers College. He was only the third black student ever to enroll at Rutgers, and the school enforced a variety of segregationist rules that barred him from many campus social events. Nonetheless, Robeson made his presence felt at the school in a variety of ways. He starred in four sports—baseball, basketball, track, and football—and was so dominant on the gridiron that he twice earned All-American honors. He was also the valedictorian of his 1919 graduating class. In his address to his fellow graduates, he called on all men and women of his generation to "make national unity a reality, at whatever sacrifice, and to provide full opportunities for the development of everyone."

After graduation, Robeson moved to Harlem, an area within New York City that was rapidly becoming known as the unofficial capital of black

America. He enrolled in law school at Columbia University. When he was not studying, he supported himself as a professional football player and postal clerk. In 1921 he married a chemist named Eslanda Cardozo Goode. Their marriage lasted forty-four years (until her death in 1965) and produced one son, Paul Jr., but it was by all accounts an unhappy one for both of them.

Robeson's rugged good looks, his athletic exploits, and his record of academic success at Rutgers ensured that his presence would be noted by Harlem's intellectual elite. Before long he was regularly being invited to gatherings at the homes of powerful and respected black leaders such as James Weldon Johnson and W.E.B. Du Bois. These evenings also gave Robeson the opportunity to meet and befriend writers, singers, and artists associated with the Harlem Renaissance, which was quickly gathering steam in the early 1920s. "In the beginning, he would sit and listen, asking questions, absorbing everything," recalled his son, Paul Jr., in Dick Russell's *Black Genius and the American Experience.* "These were the giants, men in their thirties all the way to their seventies, some of whom went back to Frederick Douglass's time."

In 1923 Robeson became the third black graduate in the history of Columbia Law School. But rather than pursuing a career in law, he instead turned his attention to the bright lights of the theatrical stage.

Controversy and Triumph

Robeson had been active in local theater and musical productions within months of his arrival in New York City, and in 1922 he had even starred in a summer production in London, England. Robeson's magnetic stage presence and his wonderful bass-baritone singing voice caught the attention of Eugene O'Neill, one of the most important playwrights in the history of American theater.

In 1924 O'Neill approached Robeson and asked him to play the lead in a new play of his called *All God's Chillun Got Wings.* Robeson was thrilled by the opportunity, but when white people learned that the play pivoted around his character's marriage to a white woman, the play became the target of a firestorm of criticism. Some New York newspapers condemned the play, a number of white politicians (including the mayor) rushed to criticize the show's content, and the Ku Klux Klan delivered a series of death threats to Robeson. Leaders within the city's black and liberal white communities rushed to defend the production, though, and their support made the play a financial triumph when it finally opened.

Robeson's emergence as a genuine theatrical star, however, did not occur until he took the title role of *Emperor Jones* in 1925. This O'Neill play gave Robeson a platform to display his great gifts as an actor, and by the time the show's run was over he had become one of America's most famous theatrical stars—white or black.

Robeson's meteoric rise to fame was further fanned by an April 1925 concert in New York's Greenwich Village in which the actor displayed his amazing singing voice. The concert, which was composed almost entirely of spirituals that Robeson had learned in his father's churches, further convinced the leaders of the Harlem Renaissance—and the wider city of New York—that a new star was being born.

Renaissance Man

Over the next several years, the multi-talented Robeson made his mark in a variety of artistic areas. He starred in the United States in theatrical productions such as *Porgy* (1928) and *Show Boat* (1928), and his moving rendition of the song "Ol' Man River" in the latter production made him and the song virtually synonymous in the minds of many American theatergoers. Other significant plays in which Robeson starred included *The Hairy Ape* (1931) and *Stevedore* (1935).

Another of Robeson's most memorable stage roles was as William Shakespeare's tormented King Othello. He first starred in *Othello* in a theatrical production in England, and in 1943 he returned to the role on Broadway. This latter version of *Othello* became the longest-running Shakespeare play in Broadway history, running for nearly 300 performances during 1943-44.

Robeson also starred in several motion pictures in the late 1920s and 1930s. His first major role was in *Body and Soul* (1924), a film by legendary African-American director Oscar Micheaux that was relegated to black movie houses. Other notable films in which he starred included *The Emperor Jones*, a 1933 movie version of the play that made him a star; *Song of Freedom* (1936); *Proud Valley* (1939); and *Tales of Manhattan* (1942).

Despite his accomplishments on stage and screen, though, Robeson's greatest fame came as a singer. During the latter half of the 1920s he made

145

repeated visits to Europe, singing before sold-out crowds in the finest auditoriums in London, Paris, and other major cities. He also became a recording star with Victor Records (later RCA Victor) and an enormously popular guest on American and European radio programs. Robeson's concerts during this period were dominated by performances of traditional black folk music and spirituals. "These songs are to Negro culture what the works of the great poets are to English culture," Robeson later wrote. "They are the soul of the race made manifest." By the late 1930s, Robeson's soulful renditions of these songs had made him one of the most popular concert singers in the world.

Cultural Scholar and Political Activist

For most of the 1930s, Robeson and his family lived primarily in London. During his time there—as well as his stints in Paris, New York City, and other cities to which he traveled—he became a serious student of world cultures. He became an expert in the history and traditions of the peoples of Africa, China, Germany, and the Soviet Union, and he eventually learned to speak fifteen languages.

During this same period, Robeson became a dedicated advocate for peace, racial equality, and economic justice. He had always been a curious and well-informed citizen of the world, but his journey into political activism did not become a turbulent one until 1934, when he toured the Soviet Union at the invitation of Soviet filmmaker Sergei Eisenstein. The Soviet authorities treated Robeson like an honored guest and made every effort to portray its Communist political system as one that rejected racism and sought to make every citizen equal to one another.

Over the next few years, Robeson repeatedly defended Soviet-style socialism as the best political system for working-class and minority peoples. He also spoke out against segregation and racial discrimination in the United States, the rise of fascism in Spain and Germany, and foreign control of Africa by European colonial governments.

When World War II erupted in Europe in 1939 Robeson returned to the United States with his family. As the war intensified and the United States became directly involved, Robeson's versions of patriotic songs such as "Ballad for Americans" and "What Is America to Me" became staples on the radio and in concert. In the meantime, though, Robeson also gave benefit concerts for progressive labor unions and walked picket lines to protest segregation. By this time, Robeson was flatly refusing to perform in any city or state where segregation was still practiced. In 1945 he received the NAACP Springarn Medal for Outstanding Achievement, possibly the most prestigious civil rights award in the country. He also cultivated friendships with personalities ranging from Chilean writer and politician Pablo Neruda and legendary boxer Joe Louis to singer Lena Horne and former First Lady Eleanor Roosevelt.

Cold War Outcast

Robeson's spectacular career came crashing down in post-World War II America. After World War II ended in 1945, the United States and the Soviet Union launched a nearly five-decade long political and military rivalry that became known as the Cold War. Fear and hatred of Communism and its supporters escalated among American lawmakers and housewives alike. By the late 1940s the U.S. House Un-American Activities Committee (HUAC), the Federal Bureau of Investigation (FBI), and numerous other Congressional committees and law enforcement agencies were seeking out Communist "agents" in every corner of American life. Any American who harbored progressive political views was at risk of being labeled a Communist and a traitor.

In 1947 this atmosphere of paranoia and fear ensnared Robeson, who was well known for his liberal political views and past praise of the Soviet Union. The first indication that he was in trouble came when several scheduled concerts were cancelled by fearful promoters. He then was called to testify several times before HUAC members who challenged his patriotism and allegiance to America.

Robeson became even more of a target in 1949, when he gave a speech in Paris at an international peace conference. During his speech, he expressed doubts that "American Negroes will go to war on behalf of those who have oppressed us for generations . . . against a country [the Soviet Union] which in one generation has raised our people to the full dignity of mankind." News of his comments were so widely condemned back in the United States that black personalities ranging from baseball star Jackie Robinson to NAACP National Secretary Walter White issued strong statements denouncing his speech.

Robeson remained defiant. He refused to acknowledge the Soviet Union's lengthening record of human rights abuses and its appalling history of state-sponsored terrorism of its own people, especially during the reign of Joseph Stalin. Scholars still debate whether his silence on these matters was due to ignorance, distrust of American news accounts of these events, or a stubborn refusal to admit that he had been wrong about Stalin and other Soviet leaders.

A Career in Tatters

By 1949 Robeson's support had shriveled down to members of the African-American community, some union organizations, and assorted other liberal groups that strongly objected to the U.S. government's treatment of the singer. Most other Americans had concluded that Robeson was "un-American." In August of that year, a scheduled Robeson concert in Peekskill, New York, had to be cancelled when members of the American Legion and the Ku Klux Klan attacked the crowd. A week later, Robeson went back to Peekskill and performed before an estimated 25,000 people. But after the crowd left to return home, many were intercepted by a mob that terrorized or savagely beat them. Local police and state troopers were on the scene, but they did nothing to stop the violence.

Robeson's fortunes continued to decline in 1950. He was banned from concert halls that only a few years ago had welcomed him with open arms, and most white media outlets refused to publish any of Robeson's statements in which he tried to defend himself. Record stores refused to carry his recordings, and in August 1950 the U.S. State Department cancelled his passport after he refused to sign an affidavit pledging that he was not a Communist (a political affiliation that was still legal in the United States). Without his passport, Robeson could no longer travel to Europe to perform. HUAC also called him to testify again. Weary and angry, Robeson lashed out at HUAC, proclaiming that "you are the real un-Americans and you should be ashamed of yourselves." Such statements were ridiculed by Senator Joseph McCarthy and other notorious Congressional leaders of the "Communist witch hunts" of the 1950s.

Fighting Back

Robeson tried to fight back. In 1950 he launched a weekly Harlem newspaper called *Freedom*. The paper operated for five years, and for much of that time Robeson contributed a regular column titled "Here Is My Story." He also continued to give concert performances, though the union halls and high school auditoriums in which he performed were a far cry from the famous concert halls that he had been singing in only a few years before. The most famous of these performances was his 1952 Peace Arch concert in Blaine, Washington, at the U.S.-Canada border. This concert, which attracted an estimated 20,000-40,000 supporters, was hastily arranged when American customs officials refused to let him cross into Canada—despite the fact that he was not legally required to have a passport to make that crossing.

In 1956 Robeson was permitted to travel to Canada for two concerts. Two years later, the U.S. State Department finally reinstated Robeson's passport. Free to leave North American soil for the first time in eight years, he performed at concerts in England and Australia. The next several years, though, were dominated by extended bouts of depression, problems with other illnesses, and extended hospital stays in Moscow and London.

In 1963 Robeson returned to the United States and moved in with a sister in Philadelphia. He lived in seclusion for the next thirteen years, refusing virtually all contact with the outside world. During this time, Robeson's former status as one of the most famous entertainers of the twentieth century was largely forgotten.

Robeson died of a stroke on December 28, 1976. His funeral service was held at a Harlem church that had for many years been led by one of his brothers, Reverend Benjamin Robeson. In 1995 Robeson was posthumously inducted into the College Football Hall of Fame.

Sources:

Boyle, Sheila Tully, and Andrew Bunie. *Paul Robeson: The Years of Promise and Achievement.* Amherst: University of Massachusetts Press, 2001.

Brown, Lloyd L. *The Young Paul Robeson: On My Journey Now.* Boulder, CO: Westview Press, 1997.

Foner, Philip S., ed. *Paul Robeson Speaks.* Secaucus, NJ: Citadel Press, 1982.

Robeson, Paul. *Here I Stand.* Boston: Beacon Press, 1958.

Russell, Dick. "All the World's Their Stage: Paul Robeson and Ira Aldridge." In *Black Genius and the American Experience.* New York: Carroll and Graf, 1998.

Bessie Smith (1894?-1937)
Singer Known as "The Empress of the Blues"

Much of her early life is shrouded in mystery, but most historians believe that Bessie Smith was born on April 15, 1894, in Chattanooga, Tennessee. Her father, William Smith, was a laborer and part-time Baptist minister who died when she was still a baby. Her mother, Laura, struggled to support Bessie and her six brothers and sisters for the next several years. She then died when Bessie was eight or nine years old, leaving Bessie's older sister Viola as the head of the household.

Viola took in laundry to keep a roof over their heads in a rough, impoverished black neighborhood of Chattanooga. Bessie was able to attend school until about eighth grade, but she could often be found performing songs on street corners with her brothers Andrew and Clarence. The modest amounts of money they earned helped put food on the family table—and gave Bessie and her brothers a taste for life in show business. When Clarence snagged a job as a singer and dancer for a touring vaudeville revue, Bessie quickly followed suit. In 1912 she joined another traveling black vaudeville company as a dancer.

Taken Under Ma Rainey's Wing

Over the next few years Smith led a nomadic existence. As part of a traveling vaudeville show, she and the other musicians, dancers, singers, and comics who performed on stage were forever on the move from one town to the next. Most of them did not earn a lot of money for their efforts, and they frequently encountered racism and segregation, both in the Jim Crow South and the northern states.

But Smith loved to perform, and she learned a great deal about show business during these years. Her main tutor was Gertrude "Ma" Rainey, one of the first great blues singers. Rainey was the star attraction in one of the touring companies for which Smith worked, and the two women became great friends. Rainey taught her young protégé how to flirt with an audience, how to recognize untrustworthy agents, promoters, and musicians, and assorted other tricks of the trade.

By the late 1910s Smith had emerged as a headliner in her own right on the vaudeville circuit. Blessed with a wonderful singing voice, she could sing everything from traditional blues and spirituals to the latest tunes from "Tin Pan Alley," the New York-based syndicate of music publishers that dominated American popular music in the early twentieth century. In addition, Smith was a skillful comedian and an exuberant dancer.

At first, some promoters were wary of featuring Smith as a star attraction. They knew that she had far darker skin and more obvious African features than most other popular black entertainers of the period. Her imposing size—she was about six feet tall and had a heavy frame—also scared off some managers and promoters who wanted a more conventionally beautiful headliner. But others looked past these factors and saw a charismatic young woman with an amazing voice. As it turned out, their faith in her star potential proved well-founded. Wherever she went, she was able to fill vaudeville tents and concert halls to capacity.

Riding the Blues to Stardom

In the early 1920s, Smith left the vaudeville circuit and became a fixture at fancy "speakeasies," private liquor-selling nightclubs that popped up all across America's cities during the Prohibition era. In 1923 she decided to stake out her career in New York City, and within weeks of her arrival she was one of the hottest tickets in the city.

Few whites even knew of her existence during her first months in Manhattan, but black New Yorkers knew all about her. They packed the concert halls and nightclubs where she performed, savoring every note she sang. "Bessie's commanding singing voice, her superb timing, and her thoroughly musical approach to even the most banal material was something no one in her field could match," wrote biographer Chris Albertson. "Her vocal material was often written by Tin Pan Alley's tunesmiths, but she reshaped their songs and charged them with joy and sorrow that appeared to be born of personal experience."

It did not take long for white New Yorkers to discover this amazing singer in their midst. In fact, Smith was but one of a host of legendary female blues singers who rose to stardom in the 1920s. Ethel Waters, Josephine Baker, Mamie Smith, Clara Smith, and Bessie's old mentor Ma Rainey all achieved new heights of popularity during this era. But only Bessie Smith earned the nickname "Empress of the Blues."

The sudden jolt of stardom that Smith and other female blues singers experienced during this time was due to two factors. First, the influx of blues and jazz music into New York City during the early 1920s coincided with an explosion of exciting poetry and literature from Harlem, the most famous black community in America. This combination of music and literature intrigued white Americans so much that Harlem became an enormously popular tourist destination. Second, the birth of the recording industry gave black blues and jazz artists the means to display their talents to people all around the country—and the world.

Legendary Songs—But No Royalties

In the early 1920s recordings by Mamie Smith and other blues singers and musicians proved that there was an untapped market for blues and jazz music. Record companies rushed to establish special divisions and record labels meant to cater specifically to black record buyers. They also sent talent scouts far and wide to find the next great recording stars.

Smith was an obvious target of record industry executives, for she was already enormously popular with black audiences. Columbia Records signed her, and on February 15, 1923, they released her first single, "Downhearted Blues" ("Gulf Coast Blues" was the song on the other side of the record). Smith's single sold more than three-quarter of a million copies in six months. It brought in so much money that it single-handedly lifted Columbia from the brink of bankruptcy. But the contract that Smith signed did not give her a penny in royalties for the record. All she received was a lump sum of $250. This blatantly unfair arrangement would be repeated again and again over the next decade, during which time Smith recorded 160 songs for Columbia. Her biggest hits included "Baby Won't You Please Come Home" (1923), "Careless Love Blues" (1925), "St. Louis Blues" (1925), "A Good Man is Hard to Find" (1928), and "Nobody Knows You When You're Down and Out" (1929).

In June 1923 Smith married a handsome night watchman named Jack Gee, who then became a manager of sorts for Smith's career (they had one adopted son, Jack Jr.). Their first years together were glamorous and luxurious.

Despite the fact that Columbia Records took ruthless advantage of Smith in the recording contracts she signed, the popularity of her records with black *and* white audiences made her an even more popular concert attraction. By 1925, she was commanding the highest performance fee of any black female singer in New York City. Smith also routinely collaborated with some of Harlem's most legendary musicians and composers, including Louis Armstrong, Benny Goodman, Joe Smith, Fletcher Henderson, and Sidney Bechet. And when she went on tour, she traveled for a time in a lavishly decorated private railcar.

Despite her growing fame among white fans that came to see her perform in Harlem and elsewhere, however, Smith never made much of an effort to be accepted by "white America." Nor did she care about black intellectuals who criticized her music and performing style as excessively crude. Smith's allegiance was to the black working-class people who had supported her since her days in vaudeville. "In her songs, Bessie Smith pretty much expressed the feelings of a generation of black listeners," explained biographer Chip Deffaa. "She might sing of unfaithful men, of financial struggles, of flooding rivers destroying homes, of the unfairness of life, of having a loved one incarcerated; she sang with understanding, forbearance, and strength. And also at times with great, spirit-lifting zest—jubilation was to be found despite adversity and oppression."

Turbulent Private Life

In many ways, the songs that Smith chose to sing in concert and in the recording studio were a reflection of her own life. Smith's repertoire was dominated by songs about casual sex, the pursuit of tasty food and strong liquor, and rebellion against those who mistreated her. These were strong elements of her personal life as well. Smith was not shy about her love for food and liquor, nor did she make much effort to hide her many sexual liaisons with men and women, even after her marriage. And she was famously demanding and hot-tempered. Smith's relationship with her husband—who also committed adultery on many occasions—was marked by episodes of violence and ugly arguments. By 1930 they were living apart, though they never bothered to get a divorce. In 1931 Smith became romantically involved with Richard Morgan. He became her primary companion for the last years of her life.

Smith's split from Gee occurred at the same time that her star, which had burned so brightly for most of the 1920s, was beginning to fade. Her voice had been closely associated with the Harlem Renaissance, but when that movement faltered, her own fortunes also sagged. The Great Depression was also a major blow to her career, and those of many other blues and jazz artists. Record sales plummeted across the country, and worried Americans dramatically curtailed their spending on concerts and other "frills."

The mid-1930s were difficult years for Smith, who could no longer command the appearance fees that she had during the height of the Harlem Renaissance. Undaunted, she decided to infuse her blues music with a dash of "swing," a lively musical trend that was sweeping the nation at the time. She seemed poised for a big comeback effort in 1937, when she accepted an invitation from promoter John Hammond to participate in "Spirituals to Swing," a huge concert event planned for New York's Carnegie Hall in 1938. On the night of September 26, 1937, however, she was killed in an automobile collision in Clarksdale, Mississippi. A huge funeral and memorial service was held for Smith several days later in Philadelphia. The following year, Hammond formally dedicated the "Spirituals to Swing" concert to her memory.

Today, Smith is regarded as one of the most influential women in the history of the blues, and there is probably no vocalist who is more closely associated with the Harlem Renaissance. Since her passing, famous black singers such as Billie Holiday and Dinah Washington have cited Smith as their greatest inspiration. In 1970 another admirer, legendary rock-and-roll singer Janis Joplin, helped pay for a headstone for Smith's grave, which had been unmarked since her burial.

Sources:

Albertson, Chris. *Bessie.* New Haven, CT: Yale University Press, 2003.

Davis, Angela Y. *Blues Legacies and Black Feminism: Gertrude "Ma" Rainey, Bessie Smith, and Billie Holiday.* New York: Pantheon Books, 1998.

Deffaa, Chip. "Bessie Smith." In *Harlem Speaks.* Edited by Cary D. Wintz. Naperville, IL: Sourcebooks, 2007.

PRIMARY SOURCES

W.E.B. Du Bois Discusses Black Hopes and Dreams

At the beginning of the twentieth century, many African Americans spent their lives trapped in a web of poverty and bigotry. The discriminatory ways of the Jim Crow South seemed destined to live on forever, and the small minority of educated African Americans despaired that the black race would ever stand on equal footing with whites.

It was in this environment that black sociologist, writer, and civil rights leader W.E.B. Du Bois published The Souls of Black Folks *in 1903. One of his most influential works,* The Souls of Black Folk *contained a series of passionate essays that explored what it meant to be a black person in America. Following is the opening chapter in the book, titled "Of Our Spiritual Strivings."*

O water, voice of my heart crying in the sand,
All night long crying with a mournful cry,
As I lie and listen, and cannot understand
The voice of my heart in my side or the voice of the sea,
O water, crying for rest, is it I, is it I?
All night long the water is crying to me.

Unresting water, there shall never be rest
Till the last moon droop and the last tide fail,
And the fire of the end begin to burn in the west;
And the heart shall be weary and wonder and cry like the
sea,
All life long crying without avail,
As the water all night long is crying to me.

—ARTHUR SYMONS

Between me and the other world there is ever an unasked question: unasked by some through feelings of delicacy; by others through the difficulty of rightly framing it. All, nevertheless, flutter round it. They approach me in a half-hesitant sort of way, eye me curiously or compassionately, and then, instead of saying directly, How does it feel to be a problem? they say, I know an excellent colored man in my town; or, I fought at Mechanicsville; or, Do not these Southern outrages make your blood boil? At these I smile, or am interested, or reduce the boiling to a simmer, as the occasion may require. To the real question, How does it feel to be a problem? I answer seldom a word.

And yet, being a problem is a strange experience,—peculiar even for one who has never been anything else, save perhaps in babyhood and in Europe. It is in the early days of rollicking boyhood that the revelation first bursts upon one, all in a day, as it were. I remember well when the shadow swept across me. I was a little thing, away up in the hills of New England, where the dark Housatonic winds between Hoosac and Taghkanic to the sea. In a wee wooden schoolhouse, something put it into the boys' and girls' heads to buy gorgeous visiting-cards—ten cents a package—and exchange. The exchange was merry, till one girl, a tall newcomer, refused my card,—refused it peremptorily, with a glance. Then it dawned upon me with a certain suddenness that I was different from the others; or like, mayhap, in heart and life and longing, but shut out from their world by a vast veil. I had thereafter no desire to tear down that veil, to creep through; I held all beyond it in common contempt, and lived above it in a region of blue sky and great wandering shadows. That sky was bluest when I could beat my mates at examination-time, or beat them at a foot-race, or even beat their stringy heads. Alas, with the years all this fine contempt began to fade; for the words I longed for, and all their dazzling opportunities, were theirs, not mine. But they should not keep these prizes, I said; some, all, I would wrest from them. Just how I would do it I could never decide: by reading law, by healing the sick, by telling the wonderful tales that swam in my head,—some way. With other black boys the strife was not so fiercely sunny: their youth shrunk into tasteless sycophancy, or into silent hatred of the pale world about them and mocking distrust of everything white; or wasted itself in a bitter cry, Why did God make me an outcast and a stranger in mine own house? The shades of the prison-house closed round about us all: walls straight and stubborn to the whitest, but relentlessly narrow, tall, and unscalable to sons of night who must plod darkly on in resignation, or beat unavailing palms against the stone, or steadily, half hopelessly, watch the streak of blue above.

After the Egyptian and Indian, the Greek and Roman, the Teuton and Mongolian, the Negro is a sort of seventh son, born with a veil, and gifted with second-sight in this American world,—a world which yields him no true self-consciousness, but only lets him see himself through the revelation of the other world. It is a peculiar sensation, this double-consciousness, this sense of always looking at one's self through the eyes of others, of measuring one's soul by the tape of a world that looks on in amused contempt and pity. One ever feels his twoness,—an American, a Negro; two souls, two thoughts, two unreconciled strivings; two warring ideals in one dark body, whose dogged strength alone keeps it from being torn asunder.

The history of the American Negro is the history of this strife,—this longing to attain self-conscious manhood, to merge his double self into a better and truer self. In this merging he wishes neither of the older selves to be lost. He would not Africanize America, for America has too much to teach the world and Africa. He would not bleach his Negro soul in a flood of white Americanism, for he knows that Negro blood has a message for the world. He simply wishes to make it possible for a man to be both a Negro and an American, without being cursed and spit upon by his fellows, without having the doors of Opportunity closed roughly in his face.

This, then, is the end of his striving: to be a co-worker in the kingdom of culture, to escape both death and isolation, to husband and use his best powers and his latent genius. These powers of body and mind have in the past been strangely wasted, dispersed, or forgotten. The shadow of a mighty Negro past flits through the tale of Ethiopia the Shadowy and of Egypt the Sphinx. Through history, the powers of single black men flash here and there like falling stars, and die sometimes before the world has rightly gauged their brightness. Here in America, in the few days since Emancipation, the black man's turning hither and thither in hesitant and doubtful striving has often made his very strength to lose effectiveness, to seem like absence of power, like weakness. And yet it is not weakness,—it is the contradiction of double aims. The double-aimed struggle of the black artisan—on the one hand to escape white contempt for a nation of mere hewers of wood and drawers of water, and on the other hand to plough and nail and dig for a poverty-stricken horde—could only result in making him a poor craftsman, for he had but half a heart in either cause. By the poverty and ignorance of his people, the Negro minister or doctor was tempted toward quackery and demagogy [arguments based on emotion or prejudice]; and by the criticism of the other world, toward ideals that made him ashamed of his lowly tasks. The would-be black savant was confronted by the paradox that the knowledge his people needed was a twice-told tale to his white neighbors, while the knowledge which would teach the white world was Greek to his own flesh and blood. The innate love of harmony and beauty that set the ruder souls of his people a-dancing and a-singing raised but confusion and doubt in the soul of the black artist; for the beauty revealed to him was the soul-beauty of a race which his larger audience despised, and he could not articulate the message of another people. This waste of double aims, this seeking to satisfy two unreconciled ideals, has wrought sad havoc with the courage and faith and deeds of ten thousand thousand people,—has sent them often wooing false gods and invoking false means of salvation, and at times has even seemed about to make them ashamed of themselves.

Away back in the days of bondage they thought to see in one divine event the end of all doubt and disappointment; few men ever worshipped Freedom with half such unquestioning faith as did the American Negro for two centuries. To him, so far as he thought and dreamed, slavery was indeed the sum of all villainies, the cause of all sorrow, the root of all prejudice; Emancipation was the key to a promised land of sweeter beauty than ever stretched before the eyes of wearied Israelites. In song and exhortation swelled one refrain—Liberty; in his tears and curses the God he implored had Freedom in his right hand. At last it came,—suddenly, fearfully, like a dream. With one wild carnival of blood and passion came the message in his own plaintive cadences:—

> "Shout, O children!
> Shout, you're free!
> For God has bought your liberty!"

Years have passed away since then,—ten, twenty, forty; forty years of national life, forty years of renewal and development, and yet the swarthy spectre sits in its accustomed seat at the Nation's feast. In vain do we cry to this our vastest social problem:—

> "Take any shape but that, and my firm nerves
> Shall never tremble!"

The Nation has not yet found peace from its sins; the freedman has not yet found in freedom his promised land. Whatever of good may have come in these years of change, the shadow of a deep disappointment rests upon the Negro people,—a disappointment all the more bitter because the unattained ideal was unbounded save by the simple ignorance of a lowly people.

The first decade was merely a prolongation of the vain search for freedom, the boon that seemed ever barely to elude their grasp,—like a tantalizing will-o'-the-wisp, maddening and misleading the headless host. The holocaust of war, the terrors of the Ku Klux Klan, the lies of carpet-baggers, the disorganization of industry, and the contradictory advice of friends and foes, left the bewildered serf with no new watchword beyond the old cry for freedom. As the time flew, however, he began to grasp a new idea. The ideal of liberty demanded for its attainment powerful means, and these the Fifteenth Amendment gave him. The ballot, which before he had looked upon as a visible sign of freedom, he now regarded as the chief means of gaining and perfecting the liberty with which war had partially endowed him. And why not? Had not votes made war and emancipated millions? Had not votes enfranchised the freedmen? Was anything impossible to a power that had done all this? A million black men started with renewed zeal to vote themselves into the kingdom. So the decade flew away, the revolution of 1876 came, and left the half-free serf weary, wondering, but still inspired. Slowly but steadily, in the following years, a new vision began gradually to replace the dream of political power,—a powerful movement, the rise of another ideal to guide the unguided, another pillar of fire by night after a clouded day. It was the ideal of "book-learning"; the curiosity, born of compulsory ignorance, to know and test the power of the cabalistic letters of the white man, the longing to know. Here at last seemed to have been discovered the mountain path to Canaan; longer than the highway of Emancipation and law, steep and rugged, but straight, leading to heights high enough to overlook life.

Up the new path the advance guard toiled, slowly, heavily, doggedly; only those who have watched and guided the faltering feet, the misty minds, the dull understandings, of the dark pupils of these schools know how faithfully, how piteously, this people strove to learn. It was weary work. The cold statistician wrote down the inches of progress here and there, noted also where here and there a foot had slipped or some one had fallen. To the tired climbers, the horizon was ever dark, the mists were often cold, the Canaan was always dim and far away. If, however, the vistas disclosed as yet no goal, no resting-place, little but flattery and criticism, the journey at least gave leisure for reflection and self-examination; it changed the child of Emancipation to the youth with dawning self-consciousness, self-realization, self-respect. In those sombre forests of his striving his own soul rose before him, and he saw himself,—darkly as through a veil; and yet he saw in himself some faint revelation of his power, of his mission. He began to have a dim feeling that, to attain his place in the world, he must be himself, and not another. For the first time he sought to analyze the burden he bore upon his back, that dead-weight of social degradation partially masked behind a half-named Negro problem. He felt his poverty; without a cent, without a home, without land, tools, or savings, he had entered into competition with rich, landed, skilled neighbors. To be a poor man is hard, but to be a poor race in a land of dollars is the very bottom of hardships. He felt the weight of his ignorance,—not simply of letters, but of life, of business, of the humanities; the accumulated sloth and shirking and awkwardness of decades and centuries shackled his hands and feet. Nor was his burden all poverty and ignorance. The red stain of bastardy, which two centuries of systematic legal defilement of Negro women had stamped upon his race, meant not only the loss of ancient African chastity, but also the hereditary weight of a mass of corruption from white adulterers, threatening almost the obliteration of the Negro home.

A people thus handicapped ought not to be asked to race with the world, but rather allowed to give all its time and thought to its own social problems. But alas! while sociologists gleefully count his bastards and his prostitutes, the very soul of the toiling, sweating black man is darkened by the shadow of a vast despair. Men call the shadow prejudice, and learnedly explain it as the natural defence of culture against barbarism, learning against ignorance, purity against crime, the "higher" against the "lower" races. To which the Negro cries Amen! and swears that to so much of this strange prejudice as is founded on just homage to civilization, culture, righteousness, and progress, he humbly bows and meekly does obeisance [gesture of deference or humility]. But before that nameless prejudice that leaps beyond all this he stands helpless, dismayed, and well-nigh speechless; before that personal disrespect and mockery, the ridicule and systematic humiliation, the distortion of fact and wanton license of fancy, the cynical ignoring of the better and the boisterous welcoming of the worse, the all-pervading desire to inculcate [implant] disdain for everything black, from Toussaint [L'Ouverture, a Haitian revolutionary leader of the 1790s] to the devil,—before this there rises a sickening despair that would disarm and discourage any nation save that black host to whom "discouragement" is an unwritten word.

But the facing of so vast a prejudice could not but bring the inevitable self-questioning, self-disparagement, and lowering of ideals which ever accompany repression and breed in an atmosphere of contempt and hate. Whisperings and portents came home upon the four winds: Lo! we are diseased and dying, cried the dark hosts; we cannot write, our voting is vain; what need of education, since we must always cook and serve? And the Nation echoed and enforced this self-criticism, saying: Be content to be servants, and nothing more; what need of higher culture for half-men? Away with the black

162

man's ballot, by force or fraud,—and behold the suicide of a race! Nevertheless, out of the evil came something of good,—the more careful adjustment of education to real life, the clearer perception of the Negroes' social responsibilities, and the sobering realization of the meaning of progress.

So dawned the time of *Sturm und Drang* [turmoil]: storm and stress to-day rocks our little boat on the mad waters of the world-sea; there is within and without the sound of conflict, the burning of body and rending of soul; inspiration strives with doubt, and faith with vain questionings. The bright ideals of the past,—physical freedom, political power, the training of brains and the training of hands,—all these in turn have waxed and waned, until even the last grows dim and overcast. Are they all wrong,—all false? No, not that, but each alone was over-simple and incomplete,—the dreams of a credulous race-childhood, or the fond imaginings of the other world which does not know and does not want to know our power. To be really true, all these ideals must be melted and welded into one. The training of the schools we need to-day more than ever,—the training of deft hands, quick eyes and ears, and above all the broader, deeper, higher culture of gifted minds and pure hearts. The power of the ballot we need in sheer self-defence,—else what shall save us from a second slavery? Freedom, too, the long-sought, we still seek,—the freedom of life and limb, the freedom to work and think, the freedom to love and aspire. Work, culture, liberty,—all these we need, not singly but together, not successively but together, each growing and aiding each, and all striving toward that vaster ideal that swims before the Negro people, the ideal of human brotherhood, gained through the unifying ideal of Race; the ideal of fostering and developing the traits and talents of the Negro, not in opposition to or contempt for other races, but rather in large conformity to the greater ideals of the American Republic, in order that some day on American soil two world-races may give each to each those characteristics both so sadly lack. We the darker ones come even now not altogether empty-handed: there are to-day no truer exponents of the pure human spirit of the Declaration of Independence than the American Negroes; there is no true American music but the wild sweet melodies of the Negro slave; the American fairy tales and folklore are Indian and African; and, all in all, we black men seem the sole oasis of simple faith and reverence in a dusty desert of dollars and smartness. Will America be poorer if she replace her brutal dyspeptic [bad-tempered] blundering with light-hearted but determined Negro humility? Or her coarse and cruel wit with loving jovial good-humor? Or her vulgar music with the soul of the Sorrow Songs?

163

Merely a concrete test of the underlying principles of the great republic is the Negro Problem, and the spiritual striving of the freedmen's sons is the travail of souls whose burden is almost beyond the measure of their strength, but who bear it in the name of an historic race, in the name of this the land of their fathers' fathers, and in the name of human opportunity.

And now what I have briefly sketched in large outline let me on coming pages tell again in many ways, with loving emphasis and deeper detail, that men may listen to the striving in the souls of black folk.

Source: Du Bois, W.E.B. "Of Our Spiritual Strivings." *The Souls of Black Folk.* Chicago: A.C. McClurg and Co., 1903.

Alain Locke Describes the Emerging Black Culture in Harlem

In the early 1920s, talented black writers such as Claude McKay, Langston Hughes, Jean Toomer, and Countee Cullen became recognized as leading literary voices of the emerging Harlem Renaissance. Taking note of their work—and the exciting black community in which most of them made their home—the editors of a popular magazine called Survey Graphic *decided to devote an entire issue to Harlem's evolving reputation as the capital of Black America.*

This special edition of Survey Graphic, *subtitled* Harlem: Mecca of the New Negro, *was published in March 1925. It was guest-edited by Alain Locke, an African-American philosopher, critic, and activist. The issue, which included contributions from McKay, Hughes, Cullen, Angelina Grimke, Rudolph Fisher, Walter F. White, and James Weldon Johnson, was a powerful collection of work that documented black feelings of hope, pride, frustration, and anger in 1920s America. The following is an excerpt from Locke's introduction to* The New Negro, *an expanded version of this special issue that was also published in 1925.*

In the last decade something beyond the watch and guard of statistics has happened in the life of the American Negro and the three norns [powers] who have traditionally presided over the Negro problem have a changeling in their laps. The Sociologist, the Philanthropist, the Race-leader are not unaware of the New Negro but they are at a loss to account for him. He simply cannot be swathed in their formulae. For the younger generation is vibrant with a new psychology; the new spirit is awake in the masses, and under the very eyes of the professional observers is transforming what has been a perennial problem into the progressive phases of contemporary Negro life.

Could such a metamorphosis have taken place as suddenly as it has appeared to? The answer is no; not because the New Negro is not here, but because the Old Negro had long become more of a myth than a man. The Old Negro, we must remember, was a creature of moral debate and historical controversy. His has been a stock figure perpetuated as an historical fiction partly in innocent sentimentalism, partly in deliberate reactionism. The Negro himself has contributed his share to this through a sort of protective social mimicry forced upon him by the adverse circumstances of dependence. So for generations in the mind of America, the Negro has been more of a formula than a human being—a something to be argued about, condemned or defended, to be "kept down," or "in his place," or "helped up," to be worried with or worried over, harassed or patronized, a social bogey or a social burden. The thinking Negro even has been induced to share this same general attitude, to focus his attention on controversial issues, to see himself in the distorted perspective of a social problem. His shadow, so to speak, has been more real to him than his personality. Through having had to appeal from the unjust stereotypes of his oppressors and traducers [spreaders of lies] to those of his liberators, friends and benefactors he has subscribed to the traditional positions from which his case has been viewed. Little true social or self-understanding has or could come from such a situation.

But while the minds of most of us, black and white, have thus burrowed in the trenches of the Civil War and Reconstruction, the actual march of development has simply flanked these positions, necessitating a sudden reorientation of view. We have not been watching in the right direction; set North and South on a sectional axis, we have not noticed the East till the sun has us blinking.

Recall how suddenly the Negro spirituals revealed themselves; suppressed for generations under the stereotypes of Wesleyan hymn harmony, secretive, half-ashamed, until the courage of being natural brought them out—and behold, there was folk-music. Similarly the mind of the Negro seems suddenly to have slipped from under the tyranny of social intimidation and to be shaking off the psychology of imitation and implied inferiority. By shedding the old chrysalis of the Negro problem we are achieving something like a spiritual emancipation. Until recently, lacking self-understanding, we have been almost as much of a problem to ourselves as we still are to others. But the decade that found us with a problem has left us with only a task. The multitude perhaps feels as yet only a strange relief and a new vague urge, but the thinking few know that in the reaction the vital inner grip of prejudice has been broken.

With this renewed self-respect and self-dependence, the life of the Negro community is bound to enter a new dynamic phase, the buoyancy from within compensating for whatever pressure there may be of conditions from without. The migrant masses, shifting from countryside to city, hurdle several generations of experience at a leap, but more important, the same thing happens spiritually in the life-attitudes and self-expression of the Young Negro, in his poetry, his art, his education and his new outlook, with the additional advantage, of course, of the poise and greater certainty of knowing what it is all about. From this comes the promise and warrant of a new leadership. As one of them has discerningly put it:

We have tomorrow
Bright before us
Like a flame.

166

Yesterday, a night-gone thing
A sun-down name.
And dawn today
Broad arch above the road we came.
We march!

This is what, even more than any "most creditable record of fifty years of freedom," requires that the Negro of today be seen through other than the dusty spectacles of past controversy. The day of "aunties," "uncles" and "mammies" is equally gone. Uncle Tom and Sambo have passed on, and even the "Colonel" and "George" play barnstorm roles from which they escape with relief when the public spotlight is off. The popular melodrama has about played itself out, and it is time to scrap the fictions, garret the bogeys and settle down to a realistic facing of facts.

First we must observe some of the changes which since the traditional lines of opinion were drawn have rendered these quite obsolete. A main change has been, of course, that shifting of the Negro population which has made the Negro problem no longer exclusively or even predominantly Southern. Why should our minds remain sectionalized, when the problem itself no longer is? Then the trend of migration has not only been toward the North and the Central Midwest, but city-ward and to the great centers of industry—the problems of adjustment are new, practical, local and not peculiarly racial. Rather they are an integral part of the large industrial and social problems of our present-day democracy. And finally, with the Negro rapidly in process of class differentiation, if it ever was warrantable to regard and treat the Negro *en masse* it is becoming with every day less possible, more unjust and more ridiculous.

In the very process of being transplanted, the Negro is becoming transformed.

The tide of Negro migration, northward and city-ward, is not to be fully explained as a blind flood started by the demands of war industry coupled with the shutting off of foreign migration, or by the pressure of poor crops coupled with increased social terrorism in certain sections of the South and Southwest. Neither labor demand, the bollweevil nor the Ku Klux Klan is a basic factor however contributory any or all of them may have been. The wash and rush of this human tide on the beach line of the northern city centers is to be explained primarily in terms of a new vision of opportunity, of social and economic freedom, of a spirit to seize, even in the face of an extortionate and heavy toil, a chance for the improvement of conditions. With each successive wave of it, the movement of the Negro becomes more and more a mass movement toward the larger and the more democratic chance—in the Negro's case a deliberate flight not only from countryside to city, but from medieval America to modern.

Take Harlem as an instance of this. Here in Manhattan is not merely the largest Negro community in the world, but the first concentration in history of so many diverse elements of Negro life. It has attracted the African, the West Indian, the Negro American; has brought together the Negro of the North and the Negro of the South; the man from the city and the man from the town and village; the peasant, the student, the business man, the professional man, artist, poet, musician, adventurer and worker, preacher and criminal, exploiter and social outcast. Each group has come with its own separate motives and for its own special ends, but their greatest experience has been the finding of one another. Proscription and prejudice have thrown these dissimilar elements into a common area of contact and interaction. Within this area, race sympathy and unity have determined a further fusing of sentiment and experience. So what began in terms of segregation becomes more and more, as its elements mix and react, the laboratory of a great race-welding. Hitherto, it must be admitted that American Negroes have been a race more in name than in fact, or to be exact, more in sentiment than in experience. The chief bond between them has been that of a common condition rather than a common consciousness; a problem in common rather than a life in common. In Harlem, Negro life is seizing upon its first chances for group expression and self-determination. It is—or promises to be—a race capital. That is why our comparison is taken with those nascent centers of folk-expression and self-determination which are playing a creative part in the world to-day. Without pretense to their political significance, Harlem has the same role to play for the New Negro as Dublin has had for the New Ireland or Prague for the New Czechoslovakia.

Harlem, I grant you, isn't typical—but it is significant, it is prophetic. No sane observer, however sympathetic to the new trend, would contend that the great masses are articulate as yet, but they stir, they move, they are more than physically restless. The challenge of the new intellectuals among them is clear enough—the "race radicals" and realists who have broken with the old epoch of philanthropic guidance, sentimental appeal and protest. But are we after all

168

only reading into the stirrings of a sleeping giant the dreams of an agitator? The answer is in the migrating peasant. It is the "man farthest down" who is most active in getting up. One of the most characteristic symptoms of this is the professional man, himself migrating to recapture his constituency after a vain effort to maintain in some Southern corner what for years back seemed an established living and clientele. The clergyman following his errant flock, the physician or lawyer trailing his clients, supply the true dues. In a real sense it is the rank and file who are leading, and the leaders who are following. A transformed and transforming psychology permeates the masses. . . .

The Negro to-day is inevitably moving forward under the control largely of his own objectives. What are these objectives? Those of his outer life are happily already well and finally formulated, for they are none other than the ideals of American institutions and democracy. Those of his inner life are yet in process of formation, for the new psychology at present is more of a consensus of feeling than of opinion, of attitude rather than of program. Still some points seem to have crystallized.

Up to the present one may adequately describe the Negro's "inner objectives" as an attempt to repair a damaged group psychology and reshape a warped social perspective. Their realization has required a new mentality for the American Negro. And as it matures we begin to see its effects; at first, negative, iconoclastic, and then positive and constructive. In this new group psychology we note the lapse of sentimental appeal, then the development of a more positive self-respect and self-reliance; the repudiation of social dependence, and then the gradual recovery from hyper-sensitiveness and "touchy" nerves, the repudiation of the double standard of judgment with its special philanthropic allowances and then the sturdier desire for objective and scientific appraisal; and finally the rise from social disillusionment to race pride, from the sense of social debt to the responsibilities of social contribution, and offsetting the necessary working and commonsense acceptance of restricted conditions, the belief in ultimate esteem and recognition. Therefore the Negro today wishes to be known for what he is, even in his faults and shortcomings, and scorns a craven and precarious survival at the price of seeming to be what he is not. He resents being spoken for as a social ward or minor, even by his own, and to being regarded a chronic patient for the sociological clinic, the sick man of American Democracy. For the same reasons he himself is through with those social nostrums and panaceas [fake or useless medicines], the so-called "solutions" of his "problem," with which he and the country have been so liberally dosed in the past. Religion, freedom, education, money—in turn, he has ardently hoped for and peculiarly trusted these things; he still believes in them, but not in blind trust that they alone will solve his life-problem.

Each generation, however, will have its creed and that of the present is the belief in the efficacy of collective efforts in race cooperation. This deep feeling of race is at present the mainspring of Negro life. It seems to be the outcome of the reaction to proscription and prejudice; an attempt, fairly successful on the whole, to convert a defensive into an offensive position, a handicap into an incentive. It is radical in tone, but not in purpose and only the most stupid forms of opposition, misunderstanding or persecution could make it otherwise. Of course, the thinking Negro has shifted a little toward the left with the world-trend, and there is an increasing group who affiliate with radical and liberal movements. But fundamentally for the present the Negro is radical on race matters, conservative on others, in other words, a "forced radical," a social protestant rather than a genuine radical. Yet under further pressure and injustice iconoclastic thought and motives will inevitably increase. Harlem's quixotic radicalisms call for their ounce of democracy today lest tomorrow they be beyond cure.

The Negro mind reaches out as yet to nothing but American wants, American ideas. But this forced attempt to build his Americanism on race values is a unique social experiment, and its ultimate success is impossible except through the fullest sharing of American culture and institutions. There should be no delusion about this. American nerves in sections unstrung with race hysteria are often fed the opiate that the trend of Negro advance is wholly separatist, and that the effect of its operation will be to encyst [enclose] the Negro as a benign foreign body in the body politic. This cannot be—even if it were desirable. The racialism of the Negro is no limitation or reservation with respect to American life; it is only a constructive effort to build the obstructions in the stream of his progress into an efficient dam of social energy and power. Democracy itself is obstructed and stagnated to the extent that any of its channels are closed. Indeed they cannot be selectively closed. So the choice is not between one way for the Negro and another way for the rest, but between American institutions frustrated on the one hand and American ideals progressively fulfilled and realized on the other. . . .

Source: Locke, Alain. "The New Negro." In *The New Negro: An Interpretation.* Edited by Alain Locke.

Poetry of the Harlem Renaissance

During the Harlem Renaissance era, African-American poets were able to showcase their talents like never before. These men and women used verse to tap into the experiences of their black ancestors and write about the hopes, dream, and frustrations of black America. In the process, these poems—as well as the novels, short stories, and plays that came out of the Renaissance— documented the resilience, dignity, and artistic talent of African Americans.

The following is a sampling of some of the themes most often explored in the poetry of the Harlem Renaissance. The first poem is Claude McKay's "If We Must Die," a famous poem of black defiance in the face of white bigotry and violence. The second and third poems are by Langston Hughes, the unofficial poet laureate of the Harlem Renaissance. "The Negro Speaks of Rivers" was the first poem published by Hughes in Crisis Magazine, and it heralded the arrival of a powerful new voice in American literature. "I, Too" showcased Hughes's belief in the rising confidence and abilities of African Americans. The fourth and fifth poems reprinted below are by Gwendolyn Bennett, one of the most talented woman writers of the Harlem Renaissance. Her poem "Hatred" focuses on the shadow of slavery and its continued impact on African Americans. "Heritage," meanwhile, is an expression of hope that African Americans will re-discover their proud African heritage. The last featured poem is "O Black and Unknown Bards!" by James Weldon Johnson, one of the leading figures of the Renaissance. Johnson's poem is both a tribute to the anonymous creators of black spirituals, and a declaration of African-American artistic talent and ambition.

"If We Must Die" by Claude McKay

If we must die, let it not be like hogs
Hunted and penned in an inglorious spot,
While round us bark the mad and hungry dogs,
Making their mock at our accursed lot.
If we must die—O let us nobly die
So that our precious blood may not be shed
In vain; then even the monsters we defy
Shall be constrained to honor us though dead!

O kinsmen! We must meet the common foe!
Though far outnumbered let us show us brave,
And for their thousand blows deal one death blow!
What though before us lies the open grave?
Like men we'll face the murderous, cowardly pack,
Pressed to the wall, dying, but fighting back!

Source: McKay, Claude. *Harlem Shadows: The Poems of Claude McKay.* New York: Harcourt, Brace and Co., 1922.

"The Negro Speaks of Rivers" by Langston Hughes

I've known rivers:
I've known rivers ancient as the world and older than the
    Flow of human blood in human veins.

My soul has grown deep like the rivers.

I bathed in the Euphrates when dawns were young.
I built my hut near the Congo and it lulled me to sleep.
I looked upon the Nile and raised the pyramids above it.
I heard the singing of the Mississippi when Abe Lincoln
    went down to New Orleans, and I've seen its muddy
    bosom turn all golden in the sunset.

I've known rivers:
Ancient, dusky rivers.

My soul has grown deep like the rivers.

Source: Hughes, Langston. *The Collected Poems of Langston Hughes.* Edited by Arnold Rampersad and David Roessel. New York: Knopf, 1994.

"I, Too" by Langston Hughes

I, too, sing America.

I am the darker brother.
They send me to eat in the kitchen
When company comes,
But I laugh,
And eat well,
And grow strong.

Tomorrow,
I'll be at the table
When company comes.
Nobody'll dare
Say to me,
"Eat in the kitchen,"
Then.

Besides,
They'll see how beautiful I am
And be ashamed—

I, too, am America.

Source: Hughes, Langston. *The Collected Poems of Langston Hughes.* Edited by Arnold Rampersad and David Roessel. New York: Knopf, 1994.

"Hatred" by Gwendolyn Bennett

I shall hate you
Like a dart of singing steel
Shot through still air
At even-tide,
Or solemnly
As pines are sober
When they stand etched

Against the sky.
Hating you shall be a game
Played with cool hands
And slim fingers.
Your heart will yearn
For the lonely splendor
Of the pine tree
While rekindled fires
In my eyes
Shall wound you like swift arrows.
Memory will lay its hands
Upon your breast
And you will understand
My hatred.

Source: Bennett, Gwendolyn. "Hatred." *Opportunity,* June 1926.

⟞⟝⟞⟝

"Heritage" by Gwendolyn Bennett

I want to see the slim palm-trees,
Pulling at the clouds
With little pointed fingers. . . .

I want to see lithe Negro girls
Etched dark against the sky
While sunset lingers.

I want to hear the silent sands,
Singing to the moon
Before the Sphinx-still face. . . .

I want to hear the chanting
Around a heathen fire
Of a strange black race.

I want to breathe the Lotus flow'r,
Sighing to the stars
With tendrils drinking at the Nile. . . .

I want to feel the surging
Of my sad people's soul,
Hidden by a minstrel-smile.

Source: Bennett, Gwendolyn. "Heritage." *Opportunity*, December 1923.

"O Black and Unknown Bards" by James Weldon Johnson

O BLACK and unknown bards of long ago,
How came your lips to touch the sacred fire?
How, in your darkness, did you come to know
The power and beauty of the minstrel's lyre?
Who first from midst his bonds lifted his eyes?
Who first from out the still watch, lone and long,
Feeling the ancient faith of prophets rise
Within his dark-kept soul, burst into song?

Heart of what slave poured out such melody
As "Steal away to Jesus"? On its strains
His spirit must have nightly floated free,
Though still about his hands he felt his chains.
Who heard great "Jordan roll"? Whose starward eye
Saw chariot "swing low"? And who was he
That breathed that comforting, melodic sigh,
"Nobody knows de trouble I see"?

What merely living clod, what captive thing,
Could up toward God through all its darkness grope.
And find within its deadened heart to sing
These songs of sorrow, love and faith, and hope?
How did it catch that subtle undertone,
That note in music heard not with the ears?
How sound the elusive reed so seldom blown,
Which stirs the soul or melts the heart to tears.

Not that great German master in his dream
Of harmonies that thundered among the stars
At the creation, ever heard a theme

Nobler than "Go down, Moses." Mark its bars
How like a mighty trumpet-call they stir
The blood. Such are the notes that men have sung
Going to valorous deeds; such tones there were
That helped make history when Time was young.

There is a wide, wider wonder in it all,
That from degraded rest and servile toil
The fiery spirit of the seer should call
These simple children of the sun and soil.
O black slave singers, gone, forgot, unfamed,
You—you alone, of all the long, long line
Of those who've sung untaught, unknown, unnamed,
Have stretched out upward, seeking the divine.

You sang not deeds of heroes or of kings;
No chant of bloody war, no exulting pean
Of arms-won triumphs; but your humble strings
You touched in chord with music empyrean.
You sting far better than you knew; the songs
That for your listeners' hungry hearts sufficed
Still live,—but more than this to you belongs;
You sang a race from wood and stone to Christ.

Source: Johnson, James Weldon, ed. *The Book of American Negro Poetry.* New York: Harcourt, Brace and Co., 1922.

James Weldon Johnson Praises the People and Spirit of Harlem

During the first three decades of the twentieth century, the New York neighborhood of Harlem became the nation's center of African-American culture. Writer and civil rights leader James Weldon Johnson, though, was one of many Harlem residents who was eager to tell black and white Americans alike that the community was composed of more than idealistic young poets, jazz and blues musicians, and residents eager to perfect the Charleston and other dance crazes of the era. According to Johnson, the elements that made Harlem a true community also included thriving churches, civic-minded fraternal organizations, and a large core of hard-working men and women "who spend their time in just about the same way that other ordinary, hard-working people do." The following is an excerpt from Black Manhattan, *Johnson's epic history of Harlem and its development into the most famous African-American community in America.*

Within the past ten years Harlem has acquired a world-wide reputation. It has gained a place in the list of famous sections of great cities. It is known in Europe and the Orient, and it is talked about by natives in the interior of Africa. It is farthest known as being exotic, colourful, and sensuous; a place of laughing, singing, and dancing; a place where life wakes up at night. This phase of Harlem's fame is most widely known because, in addition to being spread by ordinary agencies, it has been proclaimed in story and song. And certainly this is Harlem's most striking and fascinating aspect. New Yorkers and people visiting New York from the world over go to the night-clubs of Harlem and dance to such jazz music as can be heard nowhere else; and they get an exhilaration impossible to duplicate. Some of these seekers after new sensations go beyond the gay night-clubs; they nose down in under the more seamy side of things; they nose down into lower strata of life. A visit to Harlem at night—the principal streets never deserted, gay crowds skipping from one place of amusement to another, lines of taxicabs and limousines standing under the sparkling lights of the entrances to the famous night-clubs, the subway kiosks swallowing and disgorging crowds all night long—gives the impression that Harlem never sleeps and that the inhabitants thereof jazz through existence. But, of course, no one can seriously think that the two hundred thousands and more Negroes in Harlem spend their nights on any such pleasance. Of a necessity the vast majority of them are

---

ordinary, hard-working people, who spend their time in just about the same way that other ordinary, hard-working people do. Most of them have never seen the inside of a nightclub. The great bulk of them are confronted with the stern necessity of making a living, of making both ends meet, of finding money to pay the rent and keep the children fed and clothed neatly enough to attend school; their waking hours are almost entirely consumed in this unromantic task. And it is a task in which they cannot escape running up against a barrier erected especially for them, a barrier which pens them off on the morass—no, the quicksands—of economic insecurity. Fewer jobs are open to them than to any other group; and in such jobs as they get, they are subject to the old rule, which still obtains, "the last to be hired and the first to be fired."

Notwithstanding all that, gaiety is peculiarly characteristic of Harlem. The people who live there are by nature a pleasure-loving people; and though most of them must take their pleasures in a less expensive manner than in nightly visits to clubs, they nevertheless, as far as they can afford—and often much farther—do satisfy their hunger for enjoyment. And since they are constituted as they are, enjoyment being almost as essential to them as food, perhaps really a compensation which enables them to persist, it is well that they are able to extract pleasure easily and cheaply. An average group of Negroes can in dancing to a good jazz band achieve a delightful state of intoxication that for others would require nothing short of a certain per capita imbibition of synthetic gin. The masses of Harlem get a good deal of pleasure out of things far too simple for most other folks. In the evenings of summer and on Sundays they get lots of enjoyment out of strolling. Strolling is almost a lost art in New York; at least, in the manner in which it is so generally practised in Harlem. Strolling in Harlem does not mean merely walking along Lenox or upper Seventh Avenue or One Hundred and Thirty-fifth Street; it means that those streets are places for socializing. One puts on one's best clothes and fares forth to pass the time pleasantly with the friends and acquaintances and, most important of all, the strangers he is sure of meeting. One saunters along, he hails this one, exchanges a word or two with that one, stops for a short chat with the other one. He comes up to a laughing, chattering group, in which he may have only one friend or acquaintance, but that gives him the privilege of joining in. He does join in and takes part in the joking, the small talk and gossip, and makes new acquaintances. He passes on and arrives in front of one of the theatres, studies the bill for a while, undecided about going in. He finally moves on a few steps farther and joins another group and is introduced to two or three pretty girls who have just come to Harlem, perhaps only for a visit; and finds a reason to be glad that he postponed going into the theatre. The hours of a summer evening run by rapidly. This is not simply going out for a walk; it is more like going out for adventure.

In almost as simple a fashion the masses of Harlem get enjoyment out of church-going. . . . The multiplicity of churches in Harlem, and in every other Negro community, is commonly accounted for by the innate and deep religious emotion of the race. Conceding the strength and depth of this emotion, there is also the vital fact that coloured churches provide their members with a great deal of enjoyment, aside from the joys of religion. Indeed, a Negro church is for its members much more besides a place of worship. It is a social centre, it is a club, it is an arena for the exercise of one's capabilities and powers, a world in which one may achieve self-realization and preferment. Of course, a church means something of the same sort to all groups; but with the Negro all these attributes are magnified because of the fact that they are so curtailed for him in the world at large. Most of the large Harlem churches open early on Sunday morning and remain open until ten or eleven o'clock at night; and there is not an hour during that time when any one of them is empty. A good many people stay in church all day; there they take their dinner, cooked and served hot by a special committee. Aside from any spiritual benefits derived, going to church means being dressed in one's best clothes, forgetting for the time about work, having the chance to acquit oneself with credit before one's fellows, and having the opportunity of meeting, talking, and laughing with friends and of casting an appraising and approving eye upon the opposite sex. Going to church is an outlet for the Negro's religious emotions; but not the least reason why he is willing to support so many churches is that they furnish so many agreeable activities and so much real enjoyment. He is willing to support them because he has not yet, and will not have until there is far greater economic and intellectual development and social organization, any other agencies that can fill their place.

The importance of the place of the church in Negro life is not comparable with its importance among other American groups. In a community like Harlem, which has not yet attained cohesion and adjustment, the church is a stabilizing force. The integrating value of the churches in Harlem, where there are so many disintegrating forces at work, can easily be underestimated. This is especially true of churches like Mother Zion, St. Philip's, and Abyssinian, each of which is an organization with over a hundred years of continuous historical background. The severest critic of the shortcomings of the Negro church would pause before wishing a Harlem without churches. What intelligent criticism should at present insist upon is that the Negro church live more fully up to the responsibilities and opportunities which it has over and above those of the churches of other groups; that it throw out moss-back theology and obsolete dogmatics and strive to make itself a greater force in bettering the Negro's state in this world and in this country; that it seek to give out larger and larger essential values in return for the millions of dollars the Negro masses pour into its coffers. There is not now any other piece of organizational machinery that could do these things as well as the Negro church could do them. In so doing, the church would not limit, but would extend, its spiritual forces. Much higher spiritual returns could be gained by explanations to the masses of the economic factors involved in the condition of the race than by inane fulminations against dancing and theatre-going. Some ministers meet criticism of this sort by asking the critics why they do not complain as loudly about the money that Negroes spend in places of amusement as they do about the money Negroes give to the church. That is a sound question as far as it goes, but it does not go all the way. No one who spends money in a cabaret, for instance, has any right to demand of the proprietor of the place what use he proposes to make of that money; on the other hand, the church is a corporate membership institution, and those who give to its support have every right to ask about the administration of its resources. But outside criticism, however intelligent, won't go very far towards changing things; it is possible for it to have just the opposite effect; the change must be wrought from within. And it may be that there will rise up out of that element of the coloured clergy which realizes the potentialities of a modern Negro Church a man with sufficient wisdom and power to bring about a new Reformation.

In Harlem, as in all American Negro communities, the fraternal bodies also fill an important place. These fraternities, too, are in a very large degree social organizations, but they have also an economic feature. In addition to providing the enjoyment of lodge meetings, lodge balls and picnics, and the interest and excitement of lodge politics, there are provisions for taking care of the sick and burying the dead. Both of these latter provisions are highly commendable and are the means of attracting a good many members; however, the criticism can be made that very often the amount of money spent for burying the dead is out of proportion to that spent in caring for the living. Indeed, this is so general that it makes "the high cost of dying" a live question among Negroes.

Harlem is also a parade ground. During the warmer months of the year no Sunday passes without several parades. There are brass bands, marchers in resplendent regalia, and high dignitaries with gorgeous insignia riding in automobiles. Almost any excuse for parading is sufficient—the funeral of a member of the lodge, the laying of a corner-stone, the annual sermon to the order, or just a general desire to "turn out." Parades are not limited to Sundays; for when the funeral of a lodge member falls on a weekday, it is quite the usual thing to hold the exercises at night, so that members of the order and friends who are at work during the day may attend. Frequently after nightfall a slow procession may be seen wending its way along and a band heard playing a dirge that takes on a deeply sepulchral tone. But generally these parades are lively and add greatly to the movement, colour, and gaiety of Harlem. A brilliant parade with very good bands is participated in not only by the marchers in line, but also by the marchers on the sidewalks. For it is not a universal custom of Harlem to stand idly and watch a parade go by; a good part of the crowd always marches along, keeping step to the music.

Now, it would be entirely misleading to create the impression that all Harlem indulges in none other than these Arcadian-like pleasures. There is a large element of educated, well-to-do metropolitans among the Negroes of Harlem who view with indulgence, often with something less, the responses of the masses to these artless amusements. There is the solid, respectable, bourgeois class, of the average proportion, whose counterpoint is to be found in every Southern city. There are strictly social sets that go in for bridge parties, breakfast parties, cocktail parties, for high-powered cards, week-ends, and exclusive dances. Occasionally an exclusive dance is held in one of the ballrooms of a big downtown hotel. Harlem has its sophisticated, fast sets, initiates in all the wisdom of worldliness. And Harlem has, too, its underworld, its world of pimps and prostitutes, of gamblers and thieves, of illicit love and illicit liquor, of red sins and dark crimes. In a word, Harlem possesses in some degree all of the elements of a cosmopolitan centre. And by that same word, striking an average, we find that the overwhelming majority of its people are people whose counterparts may be found in any American community. Yet as a whole community it possesses a sense of humour and a love of gaiety that are distinctly characteristic.

Source: Johnson, James Weldon. *Black Manhattan*. New York: Alfred A. Knopf, 1930.

Langston Hughes Comments on Racial Identity and Artistic Integrity

In 1926 the Harlem Renaissance was in full bloom, but a philosophical divide between the lead-ing activists and writers of the movement had become evident. Some black intellectuals believed that the causes of racial equality and black social and economic advancement would be best served by African-American art and literature that emphasized the noblest qualities of the race. Others strongly disagreed. They argued that any authentic portrayal of African-American life must also acknowledge black affection for jazz and blues, describe black struggles with poverty and disillusionment, and embrace all aspects of black culture, whether whites like those aspects or not. They asserted that black artists should pursue their artistic visions without worrying about political considerations. The most eloquent and influential summary of this position was provided by Langston Hughes, one of the most gifted voices of the Renaissance, in "The Negro Artist and the Racial Mountain," which appeared in the June 23, 1926, issue of The Nation. *Following is the full text of Hughes's essay.*

One of the most promising of the young Negro poets said to me once, "I want to be a poet—not a Negro poet," meaning, I believe, "I want to write like a white poet"; meaning subconsciously, "I would like to be a white poet"; meaning behind that, "I would like to be white." And I was sorry the young man said that, for no great poet has ever been afraid of being him-self. And I doubted then that, with his desire to run away spiritually from his race, this boy would ever be a great poet. But this is the mountain standing in the way of any true Negro art in America—this urge within the race toward whiteness, the desire to pour racial individuality into the mold of American standardization, and to be as little Negro and as much American as possible.

But let us look at the immediate background of this young poet. His fami-ly is of what I suppose one would call the Negro middle class: people who are by no means rich yet never uncomfortable nor hungry—smug, contented, respectable folk, members of the Baptist church. The father goes to work every morning. He is the chief steward at a large white club. The mother sometimes does fancy sewing or supervises parties for the rich families of the town. The children go to a mixed school. In the home they read white papers and maga-zines. And the mother often says, "Don't be like niggers" when the children

---

are bad. A frequent phrase from the father is, "Look how well a white man does things." And so the word white comes to be unconsciously a symbol of all the virtues. It holds for the children beauty, morality, and money. The whisper of "I want to be white" runs silently through their minds. This young poet's home is, I believe, a fairly typical home of the colored middle class. One sees immediately how difficult it would be for an artist born in such a home to interest himself in interpreting the beauty of his own people. He is never taught to see that beauty. He is taught rather not to see it, or if he does, to be ashamed of it when it is not according to Caucasian patterns.

For racial culture the home of a self-styled "high-class" Negro has nothing better to offer. Instead there will be perhaps more aping of things white than in a less cultured or less wealthy home. The father is perhaps a doctor, lawyer, landowner, or politician. The mother may be a social worker, or a teacher, or she may do nothing and have a maid. Father is often dark but he has usually married the lightest woman he could find. The family attend a fashionable church where few really colored faces are to be found. And they themselves draw a color line. In the North they go to white theaters and white movies. And in the South they have at least two cars and a house "like white folks." Nordic manners, Nordic faces, Nordic hair, Nordic art (if any), and an Episcopal heaven. A very high mountain indeed for the would-be racial artist to climb in order to discover himself and his people.

But then there are the low-down folks, the so-called common element, and they are the majority—may the Lord be praised! The people who have their nip of gin on Saturday nights and are not too important to themselves or the community, or too well fed, or too learned to watch the lazy world go round. They live on Seventh Street in Washington or State Street in Chicago and they do not particularly care whether they are like white folks or anybody else. Their joy runs, bang! into ecstasy. Their religion soars to a shout. Work maybe a little today, rest a little tomorrow. Play awhile. Sing awhile. O, let's dance! These common people are not afraid of spirituals, as for a long time their more intellectual brethren were, and jazz is their child. They furnish a wealth of colorful, distinctive material for any artist because they still hold their own individuality in the face of American standardization. And perhaps these common people will give to the world its truly great Negro artist, the one who is not afraid to be himself. Whereas the better-class Negro would tell the artist what to do, the people at least let him alone when he does appear. And they are not ashamed of him—if they know he exists at all. And they accept what beauty is their own without question.

Certainly there is, for the American Negro artist who can escape the restrictions the more advanced among his own group would put upon him, a great field of unused material ready for his art. Without going outside his race, and even among the better classes with their "white" culture and conscious American manners, but still Negro enough to be different, there is sufficient material to furnish a black artist with a lifetime of creative work. And when he chooses to touch on the relations between Negroes and whites in this country with their innumerable overtones and undertones, surely, and especially for literature and the drama, there is an inexhaustible supply of themes at hand. To these the Negro artist can give his racial individuality, his heritage of rhythm and warmth, and his incongruous humor that so often, as in the Blues, becomes ironic laughter mixed with tears. But let us look again at the mountain.

A prominent Negro clubwoman in Philadelphia paid eleven dollars to hear Raquel Meller sing Andalusian popular songs. But she told me a few weeks before she would not think of going to hear "that woman," Clara Smith, a great black artist, sing Negro folk songs. And many an upper-class Negro church, even now, would not dream of employing a spiritual in its services. The drab melodies in white folks' hymnbooks are much to be preferred. "We want to worship the Lord correctly and quietly. We don't believe in 'shouting.' Let's be dull like the Nordics," they say, in effect.

The road for the serious black artist, then, who would produce a racial art is most certainly rocky and the mountain is high. Until recently he received almost no encouragement for his work from either white or colored people. The fine novels of Chesnutt go out of print with neither race noticing their passing. The quaint charm and humor of Dunbar's dialect verse brought to him, in his day, largely the same kind of encouragement one would give a sideshow freak (A colored man writing poetry! How odd!) or a clown (How amusing!).

The present vogue in things Negro, although it may do as much harm as good for the budding colored artist, has at least done this: it has brought him forcibly to the attention of his own people among whom for so long, unless the other race had noticed him beforehand, he was a prophet with little honor. I understand that Charles Gilpin acted for years in Negro theaters without any special acclaim from his own, but when Broadway gave him eight curtain calls, Negroes, too, began to beat a tin pan in his honor. I know a young colored writer, a manual worker by day, who had been writing well for the colored magazines for some years, but it was not until he recently broke into the white publications and his first book was accepted by a prominent New York publisher that the "best" Negroes in his city took the trouble to discover that he lived there. Then almost immediately they decided to give a grand dinner for him. But the society ladies were careful to whisper to his mother that perhaps she'd better not come. They were not sure she would have an evening gown.

The Negro artist works against an undertow of sharp criticism and misunderstanding from his own group and unintentional bribes from the whites. "O, be respectable, write about nice people, show how good we are," say the Negroes. "Be stereotyped, don't go too far, don't shatter our illusions about you, don't amuse us too seriously. We will pay you," say the whites. Both would have told Jean Toomer not to write *Cane*. The colored people did not praise it. The white people did not buy it. Most of the colored people who did read *Cane* hated it. They are afraid of it. Although the critics gave it good reviews the public remained indifferent. Yet (excepting the work of Du Bois) *Cane* contains the finest prose written by a Negro in America. And like the singing of Robeson, it is truly racial.

But in spite of the Nordicized Negro intelligentsia and the desires of some white editors we have an honest American Negro literature already with us. Now I await the rise of the Negro theater. Our folk music, having achieved world-wide fame, offers itself to the genius of the great individual American Negro composer who is to come. And within the next decade I expect to see the work of a growing school of colored artists who paint and model the beauty of dark faces and create with new technique the expressions of their own soul-world. And the Negro dancers who will dance like flame and the singers who will continue to carry our songs to all who listen—they will be with us in even greater numbers tomorrow.

Most of my own poems are racial in theme and treatment, derived from the life I know. In many of them I try to grasp and hold some of the meanings and rhythms of jazz. I am as sincere as I know how to be in these poems and yet after every reading I answer questions like these from my own people: Do you think Negroes should always write about Negroes? I wish you wouldn't read some of your poems to white folks. How do you find any thing interesting in a place like a cabaret? Why do you write about black people? You aren't black. What makes you do so many jazz poems?

But jazz to me is one of the inherent expressions of Negro life in America: the eternal tom-tom beating in the Negro soul—the tom-tom of revolt against weariness in a white world, a world of subway trains, and work, work, work; the tom-tom of joy and laughter, and pain swallowed in a smile. Yet the Philadelphia clubwoman is ashamed to say that her race created it and she does not like me to write about it. The old subconscious "white is best" runs through her mind. Years of study under white teachers, a lifetime of white books, pictures, and papers, and white manners, morals, and Puritan standards made her dislike the spirituals. And now she turns up her nose at jazz and all its manifestations—likewise almost everything else distinctly racial. She doesn't care for the Winold Reiss portraits of Negroes because they are "too Negro." She does not want a true picture of herself from anybody. She wants the artist to flatter her, to make the white world believe that all Negroes are as smug and as near white in soul as she wants to be. But, to my mind, it is the duty of the younger Negro artist, if he accepts any duties at all from outsiders, to change through the force of his art that old whispering "I want to be white," hidden in the aspirations of his people, to "Why should I want to be white? I am a Negro—and beautiful!"

So I am ashamed for the black poet who says, "I want to be a poet, not a Negro poet," as though his own racial world were not as interesting as any other world. I am ashamed, too, for the colored artist who runs from the painting of Negro faces to the painting of sunsets after the manner of the academicians because he fears the strange un-whiteness of his own features. An artist must be free to choose what he does, certainly, but he must also never be afraid to do what he might choose.

Let the blare of Negro jazz bands and the bellowing voice of Bessie Smith singing Blues penetrate the closed ears of the colored near-intellectuals until they listen and perhaps understand. Let Paul Robeson singing "Water Boy," and Rudolph Fisher writing about the streets of Harlem, and Jean Toomer holding the heart of Georgia in his hands, and Aaron Douglas drawing strange black fantasies cause the smug Negro middle class to turn from their white, respectable, ordinary books and papers to catch a glimmer of their own beauty. We younger Negro artists who create now intend to express our individual dark-skinned selves without fear or shame. If white people are pleased we are glad. If they are not, it doesn't matter. We know we are beautiful. And ugly too. The tom-tom cries and the tom-tom laughs. If colored people are pleased we are glad. If they are not, their displeasure doesn't matter either. We build our temples for tomorrow, strong as we know how, and we stand on top of the mountain, free within ourselves.

Source: Hughes, Langston. "The Negro Artist and the Racial Mountain." *The Nation,* June 23, 1926.

Frankie Manning Remembers the Savoy Ballroom

Frankie Manning was one of the leading dancers and choreographers of the Harlem Renaissance era. During the 1930s and 1940s Manning and other members of a dance troupe known as Whitey's Lindy Hoppers traveled throughout North America and Europe. Manning became known as the unofficial "Ambassador of the Lindy Hop" during that time.

Manning started dancing in his early teens at Harlem dance halls. He eventually became a star performer at the Savoy Ballroom, one of Harlem's most famous and glamorous clubs. In 1935 Manning and other top Savoy dancers were enlisted by producer Herbert White to join the Whitey's Lindy Hoppers dance group. It was at this point that Manning created the first ensemble Lindy Hop dance routines and launched his stellar career as a choreographer. In the following interview for the PBS documentary series "Jazz," Manning recalls how he felt the very first time he set foot on the dance floor at the Savoy Ballroom.

Question: Tell me what you felt the first time you went into the Savoy . . . ?

Frankie: . . . I always knew about the Savoy Ballroom because I used to go to the Outhammer Ballroom, and I went to the Renaissance Ballroom. And there was a group of us, were friends that we were always together and we always went to dances together and our one ambition was to go the Savoy Ballroom, you know. So we say, "Well, OK. Let's go to the Savoy Ballroom, but we can't go alone. Because if you go by yourself, nobody's going to dance with you." So, we were, we went up there as a group. And I remember it was six of us. And we're walking up these steps, and as we're climbing up the steps I could hear this music coming down, you know, and as the music is coming down the stairway, stairwell, we're walking up there and we started, "Oh man you hear that music!" "Wow!!" And we walked through the door. We opened the door and we turned around. As you come up the steps, when you come through the doors, your back is to the bandstand. So, you turn around [in] the stairwell, and then you face the band. And as I turn around and face this, the floor was full of people. And it looked like everyone on the floor was doing the Lindy Hop. I don't say that they were, but that's the way it seemed to me, like everybody was just bouncing up and down and the music was romping and stomping and we were, we started, "Man!" We started looking at each other, "Hey man you hear this music!" "Look at all these people in

---

Archival material supplied by WETA-TV, Washington D.C.

this place dancing and jumpin'!" And the floor was, oh. Looked like the floor was getting into the mood of dance 'cause the floor was just bouncing up and down, you know, and the people were bouncing up and down and Chick Webb was on the bandstand whalin', you know. . . .

Then we walked over to the bandstand and Chick Webb was swinging out there, and we said, "Oh, man . . . . I have never seen anything or heard anything like this." Although we'd been to all the other ballrooms in Harlem, this was our first time in the Savoy, and it was such a wonderful moment in my life, to go in the Savoy and listen to the band swinging and watch those people dancing out there and we walked over to one corner and there was like a circle, you know, people had formed a circle and were some dancers was dancing in the circle, you know, and we were watching those, those guys dancing and we looked at each other, say, "Man, we can't dance over here (laughs), 'cause these guys are too good. We better go down the other side where . . ." Now, in the Savoy Ballroom, I'd like to explain to you. Savoy Ballroom had two bandstands side by side, and they would have, like, on the northern side of the ballroom, the northern side, a bandstand was the number one band, which was Chick Webb's band. And now on the other side, with the south side bandstand, was Teddy Hill's band. Now, these are two big jazz bands. They had thirteen pieces. Each band had thirteen pieces, and what, what would happen is that Chick Webb would be playing, you know? And when it's come time for his break, he'd be playing this song, Teddy Hill's band is coming on to the stage. They would sit down on the stage and they would pick up the music where Chick Webb was playing. So, now you got two bands playing at the same time, and then, Chick Webb's band would kind of fade out and Teddy Hill's band pick up. And then, everybody'd start dancing temp, so it was continuous music. And, I had never . . . Boy, it was just such a wonderful time in, in our life, you know, to come up there, you know, as youngsters and, and be exposed to this kind of music. Oh, wow!"

Source: Interview with Norma Miller and Frankie Manning, June 26, 1997. From *Jazz: A Film by Ken Burns*. Available online at www.pbs.org/jazz/about/about_transcripts.htm.

Dorothy West Recalls Amateur Night at Harlem's Apollo Theatre

The talented short story writer and poet Dorothy West was devoted to the ideals of the Harlem Renaissance, and she fought to keep the movement alive long after many other Renaissance voices drifted away. In 1934, for example, she launched the African-American literary magazine Challenge in an unsuccessful effort to revive the fading literary output of the movement. For much of the Great Depression, she also wrote essays and short stories about black life in America for the Works Progress Administration's Federal Writers Project (FWP). The following essay written for the FWP describes her impressions of an evening at Harlem's famed Apollo Theater in November 1938, long after the heyday of the Renaissance. West's account of this particular "amateur night" at the Apollo implies that she and others who believed that the Harlem Renaissance would usher in a new age of racial equality and harmony were mistaken. As West makes poignantly clear, the "race problem" remains an ugly reality in America.

The second balcony is packed. The friendly, familiar usher who scowls all the time without meaning it flatfoots up and down the stairs trying to find seats for the sweethearts. Through his tireless manipulation, separated couples are reunited, and his pride is pardonable.

The crowd has come early, for it is amateur night. The Apollo Theatre is full to overflowing. Amateur night is an institution. Every Wednesday, from eleven until midnight, the hopeful aspirants come to the mike, lift up their voices and sing, and retire to the wings for the roll call, when a fluttering piece of paper dangled above their heads comes to rest—determined by the volume of applause—to indicate to whom the prizes shall go.

The box seats are filled with sightseeing whites led in tow by swaggering blacks. The floor is chocolate liberally sprinkled with white sauce. But the balconies belong to the hard-working, holidaying Negroes, and the jitterbug whites are intruders, and their surface excitement is silly compared to the earthy enjoyment of the Negroes.

The moving picture ends. The screen shoots out of sight. The orchestra blares out the soul-ticking tune, "I Think You're Wonderful, I Think You're Grand."

Spontaneously, feet and hands beat out the rhythm, and the show is on. The regular stage show precedes Amateur Hour. Tonight an all-girls orchestra dominates the stage. A long black girl in flowing pink blows blue notes out of a clarinet. It is a hot song, and the audience stomps its approval. A little yellow trumpeter swings out. She holds a high note, and it soars up solid. The fourteen pieces are in the groove.

The comedians are old-timers. Their comedy is pure Harlemese, and their prototypes are scattered throughout the audience. There is a burst of appreciative laughter and a round of applause when the redoubtable Jackie "Moms" Mabley states that she is doing general housework in the Bronx and adds, with telling emphasis, "When you do housework up there, you really do housework."

Next, a real idiom of Negroes is displayed when one comedian observes to another, who is carrying a fine fur coat for his girl, "Anytime I see you with something on your arm, somebody is without something."

The show moves on. The Sixteen girls of sixteen varying shades dance without precision but with effortless joy. The best of their spontaneous steps will find their way downtown. A long brown boy who looks like Cab Calloway sings, "Papa Tree-Top Tall," ending the regular stage show. The acts file onstage. The chorus girls swing in the background. It is a free-for-all, and the familiar theme song is playing. The black-face comic grabs the prettiest chorine and they truck on down. When the curtain descends, both sides of the house are having fun.

A Negro show would rather have the plaudits of an Apollo audience than any other applause. For the Apollo is the hard testing ground of Negro show business, and approval there can make or break an act.

It is eleven now. The house lights go up. The audience is restless and expectant. Somebody has brought a whistle that sounds like a wailing baby. The cry fills the theater and everybody laughs. The orchestra breaks into the theater's theme song again. The curtain goes up. A radio announcer talks into a mike, explaining to his listeners that the three hundred and first broadcast of Amateur Hour at the Apollo is on the air. He signals to the audience and they obligingly applaud.

The emcee comes out of the wings. The audience knows him. He is Negro to his toes, but even Hitler would classify him as Aryan at first glance. He begins a steady patter of jive. When the audience is ready and mellow, he calls the first amateur out of the wings.

Willie comes out and, on his way to the mike, touches the Tree of Hope. For several years the original Tree of Hope stood in front of the Lafayette Theatre on Seventh Avenue until the Commissioner of Parks tore it down. It was believed to bring good fortune to whatever actor touched it, and some say it was not the Parks Department that cut it down, but the steady stream of down-and-out actors since the Depression years who wore it out.

Willie sings "I Surrender Dear" in a pure Georgia accent. "I can' mak' mah way," he moans. The audience hears him out and claps kindly. He bows and starts for the wings. The emcee admonishes, "You got to boogie-woogie off the stage, Willie." He boogie-woogies off, which is as much a part of establishment ritual as touching the Tree of Hope.

Vanessa is next. She is black and the powder on her face makes her look purple. She is dressed in black, and is altogether unprepossessing. She is the kind of singer who makes faces and regards a mike as an enemy to be wrestled with. The orchestra sobs out her song, "I Cried for You," and she says, "Now it's your turn to cry over me." Vanessa is an old-time "coon shouter." She wails and moans deep blue notes. The audience gives her their highest form of approval. They clap their hands in time with the music. She finishes to tumultuous applause and accepts their approval with proud self-confidence. To their wild delight, she flings her arms around the emcee, and boogie-woogies off with him.

Ida comes out in a summer print dress to sing that beautiful lyric, "I Let a Song Go Out of My Heart," in a nasal, off-key whine. Samuel follows her. He is big and awkward, and his voice is very earnest as he promises, "I Won't Tell a Soul I Love You." They are both so inoffensive and sincere that the audience lets them off with light applause.

Coretta steps to the mike next. Her first note is so awful, the emcee goes to the Tree of Hope and touches it for her. The audience lets her sing the first bar, then bursts into catcalls and derisive whistling. In a moment the familiar police siren is heard offstage, and big, dark brown "Porto Rico," who is part and parcel of amateur night, comes onstage with nothing covering his nakedness but a brassiere and panties and shoots twice at Coretta's feet with a stunt gun filled with blanks. She hurriedly retires to the wings with Porto Rico switching after her, brandishing his gun.

A lean dark boy playing a clarinet pours out such sweetness in "Body and Soul" that somebody rises and shouts, "Peace, brother!" in heartfelt approval.

Margaret follows with a sour note. She has chosen to sing "Old Folks," and her voice quavers so from stage fright that her song becomes an unfortunate choice, and the audience stomps for Porto Rico who appears in a pink and blue ballet costume to run her off the stage.

David is next on the program. With mounting frenzy he sings the intensely pleading blues song, "Rock It for Me." He clutches his knees, rolls his eyes, sings away from the mike, and works himself up to a pitch of excitement that is only cooled by the appearance of Porto Rico in a red brassiere, an ankle-length red skirt, and an exaggerated hat. The audience goes wild.

Ida comes out. She is a lumpy girl in a salmon pink blouse. The good-looking emcee leads her to the mike and pats her shoulder encouragingly. She snuggles up to him, and a female onlooker audibly snorts, "She sure wants to be hugged." A male spectator shouts, gleefully, "Give her something!"

Ida sings the plaintive, "My Reverie." Her accent is late West Indian and her voice is so bad, for a minute you wonder if it's an act. Instantly there are whistles, boos, and handclapping. The siren sounds offstage and Porto Rico rushes in wearing an old-fashioned corset and a marabou-trimmed bed jacket. His shots leave her undisturbed. The audience tries to drown her out with louder applause and whistling. She holds to the mike and sings to the bitter end. It is Porto Rico who trots sheepishly after her when she walks unabashed from the stage.

James comes to the mike and is reminded by the audience to touch the Tree of Hope. He hasn't forgotten. He tries to start his song, but the audience will not let him. The emcee explains to him that the Tree of Hope is a sacred emblem. The boy doesn't care, and begins his song again. He has been in New York two days, and the emcee cracks that he's been in New York two days too long. The audience refuses to let the lad sing, and the emcee banishes him to the wings to think it over.

A slight, young girl in a crisp white blouse and neat black skirt comes to the mike to sing "Itisket, Itasket?" She has lost her yellow basket, and her listeners spontaneously inquire of her, "Was it red?" She shouts back dolefully, "No, no, no, no!" "Was it blue?" No, it wasn't blue, either. They go on searching together.

A chastened James reappears and touches the Tree of Hope. A woman states with grim satisfaction, "He teched de tree dat time." He has tried to upset a precedent, and the audience is against him from the start. They boo and whistle immediately. Porto Rico in red flannels and a floppy red hat happily shoos him off the stage.

A high school girl in middy blouse, jumper, and socks rocks "Froggy Bottom." She is the youngest thing yet, and it doesn't matter how she sings. The house rocks with her. She winds up triumphantly with a tap dance, and boogie-woogies confidently off the stage.

A frightened lad falls upon the mike. It is the only barrier between him and the murderous multitude. The emcee's encouragement falls on frozen ears. His voice starts down in his chest and stays here. The house roars for the kill; Porto Rico, in a baby's bonnet and a little girl's party frock, finishes him off with dispatch.

A white man comes out of the wings, but nobody minds. They have got accustomed to occasional white performers at the Apollo. There was a dancing act in the regular stage show that received deserved applause. The emcee announces the song, "That's Why"—he omits the next word—"Were Born." He is a Negro emcee. He will not use the word *darky* in announcing a song a white man is to sing.

The white man begins to sing, "Someone had to plow the cotton, Someone had to plant the corn, Someone had to work while the white folks played, That's why darkies were born." The Negroes hiss and boo. Instantly the audience is partisan. The whites applaud vigorously. But the greater volume of hisses and boos drown out the applause. The singer halts. The emcee steps to the house mike and raises his hand for quiet. He does not know what to say, and says ineffectually that the song was written to be sung and urges that the singer be allowed to continue. The man begins again, and on the instant is booed down. The emcee does not know what to do. They are on a sectional hookup and the announcer has welcomed Boston and Philadelphia to the program during the station break. The studio officials, the listening audience, largely white, has heard a Negro audience booing a white man. It is obvious that in his confusion the emcee has forgotten what the song connotes. The Negroes are not booing the white man as such. They are booing him for his categorization of them. The song is not new. A few seasons ago they listened to it in silent resentment. Now they have learned to vocalize their bitterness. They cannot bear that a white man, as poor as themselves, should so separate himself from their common fate and sing paternally for a price of their predestined lot to serve.

For a third time the man begins, and now all the fun that has gone before is forgotten. There is resentment in every heart. The white man will not save the situation by leaving the stage, and the emcee steps again to the house mike with an impassioned plea. The Negroes know this emcee. He is as white as any white man. Now it is ironic that he should be so fair, for the difference between him and the amateur is too undefined. The emcee spreads out his arms and begins, "My people—" he says without explanation that "his people" should be proud of the song. He begs "his people" to let the song be sung to show that they are ladies and gentlemen. He winds up with a last appeal to "his people" for fair play. He looks for all the world like the plantation owner's yellow boy acting as buffer between the blacks and the big house.

The whole house breaks into applause, and this time the scattered hisses are drowned out. The amateur begins and ends in triumph. He is the last contestant, and in the line-up immediately following, he is overwhelmingly voted first prize. More of the black man's blood money goes out of Harlem.

The show is over. The orchestra strikes up, "I Think You're Wonderful." The audience files out. They are quiet and confused and sad. It is twelve on the dot. Six hours of sleep and then back to the Bronx or up and down an elevator shaft. Yessir, Mr. White Man, I work all day while you-all play. It's only fair. That's why darkies were born.

Source: West, Dorothy. "Amateur Night in Harlem." *American Life Histories: Manuscripts from the Federal Writers' Project, 1936-1940.* Washington, DC: Library of Congress, Manuscript Division, WPA Federal Writers' Project Collection, 1889-1942.

Langston Hughes Remembers the Harlem Renaissance

Langston Hughes, the most famous writer of the Harlem Renaissance, was fully aware of the tangled emotions and expectations that the movement created, not only in Harlem but across all of black America. Hughes was an eyewitness to every aspect of life in Harlem during the Renaissance. He frequented the glitzy jazz nightclubs that also attracted hordes of white patrons, and he attended fancy Harlem dinner parties where black poets and intellectuals rubbed shoulders with their white counterparts. But Hughes refused to turn away from the parts of Harlem where marquee lights did not shine, such as the grim apartment blocks where countless black families continued to wage a daily battle against poverty and bigotry. In the following excerpt from his autobiography The Big Sea, *Hughes captures both the excitement and the disillusionment that swirled around the streets of Harlem during the extraordinary Renaissance era.*

The 1920's were the years of Manhattan's black Renaissance. It began with *Shuffle Along, Running Wild,* and the Charleston. Perhaps some people would say even with *The Emperor Jones,* Charles Gilpin, and the tom-toms at the Provincetown. But certainly it was the musical revue, *Shuffle Along,* that gave a scintillating send-off to that Negro vogue in Manhattan, which reached its peak just before the crash of 1929, the crash that sent Negroes, white folks, and all rolling down the hill toward the Works Progress Administration.

Shuffle Along was a honey of a show. Swift, bright, funny, rollicking, and gay, with a dozen danceable, singable tunes. Besides, look who were in it: The now famous choir director, Hall Johnson, and the composer, William Grant Still, were a part of the orchestra. Eubie Blake and Noble Sissle wrote the music and played and acted in the show. Miller and Lyles were the comics. Florence Mills skyrocketed to fame in the second act. Trixie Smith sang "He May Be Your Man But He Comes to See Me Sometimes." And Caterina Jarboro, now a European prima donna, and the internationally celebrated Josephine Baker were merely in the chorus. Everybody was in the audience—including me. People came back to see it innumerable times. It was always packed.

To see *Shuffle Along* was the main reason I wanted to go to Columbia. When I saw it, I was thrilled and delighted. From then on I was in the gallery of the Cort Theatre every time I got a chance. That year, too, I saw Katharine

Cornell in *A Bill of Divorcement*, Margaret Wycherly in *The Verge*, Maugham's *The Circle* with Mrs. Leslie Carter, and the Theatre Guild production of Kaiser's *From Morn Till Midnight*. But I remember *Shuffle Along* best of all. It gave just the proper push—a pre-Charleston kick—to that Negro vogue of the 20's, that spread to books, African sculpture, music, and dancing.

Put down the 1920's for the rise of Roland Hayes, who packed Carnegie Hall, the rise of Paul Robeson in New York and London, of Florence Mills over two continents, of Rose McClendon in Broadway parts that never measured up to her, the booming voice of Bessie Smith and the low moan of Clara on thousands of records, and the rise of that grand comedienne of song, Ethel Waters, singing: "Charlie's elected now! He's in right for sure!" Put down the 1920's for Louis Armstrong and Gladys Bentley and Josephine Baker.

White people began to come to Harlem in droves. For several years they packed the expensive Cotton Club on Lenox Avenue. But I was never there, because the Cotton Club was a Jim Crow club for gangsters and monied whites. They were not cordial to Negro patronage, unless you were a celebrity like Bojangles. So Harlem Negroes did not like the Cotton Club and never appreciated its Jim Crow policy in the very heart of their dark community. Nor did ordinary Negroes like the growing influx of whites toward Harlem after sundown, flooding the little cabarets and bars where formerly only colored people laughed and sang, and where now the strangers were given the best ringside tables to sit and stare at the Negro customers—like amusing animals in a zoo.

The Negroes said: "We can't go downtown and sit and stare at you in your clubs. You won't even let us in your clubs." But they didn't say it out loud—for Negroes are practically never rude to white people. So thousands of whites came to Harlem night after night, thinking the Negroes loved to have them there, and firmly believing that all Harlemites left their houses at sundown to sing and dance in cabarets, because most of the whites saw nothing but the cabarets, not the houses.

Some of the owners of Harlem clubs, delighted at the flood of white patronage, made the grievous error of barring their own race, after the manner of the famous Cotton Club. But most of these quickly lost business and folded up, because they failed to realize that a large part of the Harlem attraction for downtown New Yorkers lay in simply watching the colored customers amuse themselves. And the smaller clubs, of course, had no big floor

197

shows or a name band like the Cotton Club, where Duke Ellington usually held forth, so, without black patronage, they were not amusing at all.

Some of the small clubs, however, had people like Gladys Bentley, who was something worth discovering in those days, before she got famous, acquired an accompanist, specially written material, and conscious vulgarity. But for two or three amazing years, Miss Bentley sat, and played a big piano all night long, literally all night, without stopping—singing songs like "The St. James Infirmary," from ten in the evening until dawn, with scarcely a break between the notes, sliding from one song to another, with a powerful and continuous underbeat of jungle rhythm. Miss Bentley was an amazing exhibition of musical energy—a large, dark, masculine lady, whose feet pounded the floor while her fingers pounded the keyboard—a perfect piece of African sculpture, animated by her own rhythm.

But when the place where she played became too well known, she began to sing with an accompanist, became a star, moved to a larger place, then downtown, and is now in Hollywood. The old magic of the woman and the piano and the night and the rhythm being one is gone. But everything goes, one way or another. The '20s are gone and lots of fine things in Harlem night life have disappeared like snow in the sun—since it became utterly commercial, planned for the downtown tourist trade, and therefore dull.

The lindy-hoppers at the Savoy even began to practice acrobatic routines, and to do absurd things for the entertainment of the whites, that probably never would have entered their heads to attempt merely for their own effortless amusement. Some of the lindy-hoppers had cards printed with their names on them and became dance professors teaching the tourists. Then Harlem nights became show nights for the Nordics.

Some critics say that that is what happened to certain Negro writers, too—that they ceased to write to amuse themselves and began to write to amuse and entertain white people, and in so doing distorted and over-colored their material, and left out a great many things they thought would offend their American brothers of a lighter complexion. Maybe—since Negroes have writer-racketeers, as has any other race. But I have known almost all of them, and most of the good ones have tried to be honest, write honestly, and express their world as they saw it.

All of us know that the gay and sparkling life of the so-called Negro Renaissance of the '20's was not so gay and sparkling beneath the surface as it looked. Carl Van Vechten, in the character of Byron in *Nigger Heaven*, captured some of the bitterness and frustration of literary Harlem that Wallace Thurman later so effectively poured into his *Infants of the Spring*—the only novel by a Negro about that fantastic period when Harlem was in vogue.

It was a period when, at almost every Harlem upper-crust dance or party, one would be introduced to various distinguished white celebrities there as guests. It was a period when almost any Harlem Negro of any social importance at all would be likely to say casually: 'As I was remarking the other day to Heywood—,' meaning [journalist] Heywood Broun. Or: 'As I said to George—,' referring to [composer] George Gershwin. It was a period when local and visiting royalty were not at all uncommon in Harlem. And when the parties of A'Lelia Walker, the Negro heiress, were filled with guests whose names would turn any Nordic social climber green with envy. It was a period when Harold Jackman, a handsome young Harlem school teacher of modest means, calmly announced one day that he was sailing for the Riviera for a fortnight, to attend Princess Murat's yachting party. It was a period when Charleston preachers opened up shouting churches as sideshows for white tourists. It was a period when at least one charming colored chorus girl, amber enough to pass for a Latin American, was living in a penthouse, with all her bills paid by a gentleman whose name was banker's magic on Wall Street. It was a period when every season there was at least one hit play on Broadway acted by a Negro cast. And when books by Negro authors were being published with much greater frequency and much more publicity than ever before or since in history. It was a period when white writers wrote about Negroes more successfully (commercially speaking) than Negroes did about themselves. It was the period (God help us!) when Ethel Barrymore appeared in blackface in *Scarlet Sister Mary!* It was the period when the Negro was in vogue.

I was there. I had a swell time while it lasted. But I thought it wouldn't last long. (I remember the vogue for things Russian, the season the Chauve-Souris first came to town.) For how could a large and enthusiastic number of people be crazy about Negroes forever? But some Harlemites thought the millennium had come. They thought the race problem had at last been solved through Art plus Gladys Bentley. They were sure the New Negro would lead a new life from then on in green pastures of tolerance created by Countee Cullen, Ethel Waters, Claude McKay, Duke Ellington, Bojangles, and Alain Locke.

I don't know what made any Negroes think that—except that they were mostly intellectuals doing the thinking. The ordinary Negroes hadn't heard of the Negro renaissance. And if they had, it hadn't raised their wages any. As for all those white folks in the speakeasies and night clubs of Harlem—well, maybe a colored man could find *some* place to have a drink that the tourists hadn't yet discovered.

Source: Hughes, Langston. *The Big Sea: An Autobiography.* New York: Hill and Wang, 1940.

IMPORTANT PEOPLE, PLACES, AND TERMS

Afrophiles
Black slang term for wealthy white supporters of Harlem Renaissance artists and writers.

Bennett, Gwendolyn (1902-1981)
Writer, painter, and educator who also served as an editor at *Opportunity*.

Bentley, Gladys (1907-1960)
Singer and entertainer during the final years of the Harlem Renaissance.

Blues
An African-American musical genre founded on the topical themes and repetitive rhythms of slavery-era spirituals and work songs.

Bontemps, Arna (1902-1972)
Novelist, poet, and anthologist.

Brown, Sterling (1901-1989)
Scholar, folklorist, and author of the 1932 poetry collection *Southern Road*.

Calloway, Cab (1907-1994)
Jazz singer and bandleader.

Cotton Club
A glamorous nightclub in Harlem that owed its popularity at least in part to blatantly racist employment and admittance policies.

The Crisis
Literary magazine of the NAACP during the Harlem Renaissance.

Cullen, Countee (1903-1946)
Poet and novelist who ranked as one of the most acclaimed writers of the Renaissance.

Douglas, Aaron (1898-1979)
The most prominent painter of the Harlem Renaissance era.

Du Bois, W.E.B. (1868-1963)
Civil rights leader, scholar, essayist, novelist, and long-time managing editor of *The Crisis*.

Ellington, Duke (1899-1974)
Pianist, composer, and bandleader of the Duke Ellington Orchestra.

Fauset, Jessie Redmon (1882?-1961)
Novelist and poet who advanced the careers of many other writers as an editor of *The Crisis*.

Fisher, Rudolph (1897-1934)
Musician, physician, and novelist.

Garvey, Marcus (1887-1940)
Jamaican native who became a leading voice of black nationalism in America in the World War I era.

Gentrification
Restoration of impoverished inner city neighborhoods and areas by middle- and upper-class investors, businesspeople, and home buyers.

Gilpin, Charles (1878-1930)
Stage actor who starred in the famous 1920 production of *The Emperor Jones*.

Henderson, Fletcher (1897-1952)
Influential record executive, composer, and bandleader.

Hughes, Langston (1902-1967)
Novelist, playwright, and essayist who was also known as the "poet laureate" of the Renaissance.

Hurston, Zora Neale (1891-1960)
Novelist, playwright, folklorist, and anthropologist.

Jazz
A musical form that incorporates elements of blues and ragtime, with an emphasis on musical improvisation.

Jim Crow

Post-Reconstruction laws that codified segregation and discrimination against African Americans in virtually all aspects of daily life across the South.

Johnson, Charles S. (1893-1956)

Educator and sociologist who also served as managing editor of *Opportunity.*

Johnson, James Weldon (1871-1938)

Novelist, poet, journalist, lyricist, and diplomat who also led the NAACP during the height of the Harlem Renaissance.

Jungle Alley

Nickname for a stretch of 133rd Street in southern Harlem that housed numerous popular nightclubs and cabarets.

Larsen, Nella (1891-1936)

Author of *Quicksand* and *Passing,* two of the finest novels of the Harlem Renaissance.

Locke, Alain (1885-1954)

Scholar and editor who was a leading architect of the literary branch of the Harlem Renaissance.

Mason, Charlotte Osgood (1854-1946)

Wealthy white patron of Langston Hughes and other leading writers of the Harlem Renaissance.

McKay, Claude (1889-1948)

Poet and novelist who produced some of the best-known literary works of the Renaissance.

Mills, Florence (1895-1927)

Singer and entertainer who starred in the 1921 musical *Shuffle Along.*

National Association for the Advancement of Colored People (NAACP)

Founded in 1909, the most prominent civil rights organization in U.S. history.

National Urban League (NUL)

A leading African-American civil rights organization, founded in New York in 1910.

New Negro

Term used to describe African Americans of the early twentieth century who were proud of their ethnic heritage, ambitious and educated, and determined to attack racist aspects of American society.

Nordic

African-American slang term for whites.

Opportunity

Magazine published by the National Urban League during the Harlem Renaissance era.

Ragtime

A form of jazz music played in syncopated or ragged time, often traced back to the call-and-response patterns of slave work songs.

Rainey, Gertrude "Ma" (1886-1939)

Influential blues singer of the 1910s and 1920s.

Reconstruction

The post-Civil War era (1865-1877) during which federal authorities tried to reorganize the society and political structure of the South to expand the civil rights of African Americans.

Robeson, Paul (1898-1976)

Athlete, singer, actor, and political activist.

Savage, Augusta (1892-1962)

Sculptor and teacher.

Savoy Ballroom

One of the most famous New York nightclubs of the Harlem Renaissance era.

Schomberg, Arthur (1874-1938)

Writer, scholar, and curator whose African-American literature collection became the foundation for the Schomberg Center for Research in Black Culture in New York City.

Segregation

The practice of formally separating non-whites from whites in such areas as schools, restaurants, housing, and other social and cultural settings.

Separatism

A belief that ethnic groups should be separated or segregated from one another.

Smith, Bessie (1894?-1937)

Famous blues singer of the Renaissance era.

Speakeasy

Illegal drinking establishment of the Prohibition era.

Thurman, Wallace (1902-1934)

Novelist and journalist who founded and edited the influential literary magazine *Fire!!*

Toomer, Jean (1894-1967)

Poet, playwright, and author of the acclaimed experimental novel *Cane*.

Van Der Zee, James (1886-1983)

Musician and photographer.

Van Vechten, Carl (1880-1964)

White novelist and supporter of the Harlem Renaissance.

Washington, Booker T. (1856-1915)

Prominent African-American educator and activist of the late nineteenth and early twentieth centuries.

Waters, Ethel (1896-1977)

Singer and actress.

White, Walter F. (1893-1955)

Novelist, historian, and civil rights leader who served as executive secretary of the NAACP from 1931 to 1955.

CHRONOLOGY

Note: This Chronology of Events includes a see reference feature. These references refer readers to sections of the Narrative Overview where the events are discussed in greater depth.

1865

The Civil War ends and the twelve-year period known as Reconstruction begins, forcing Southern states to end a wide range of discriminatory practices against blacks. *See p. 7.*

1868

The Fourteenth Amendment to the U.S. Constitution becomes law, granting citizenship to African Americans. *See p. 7.*

1870

The Fifteenth Amendment to the U.S. Constitution is ratified, guaranteeing black voting rights. *See p. 7.*

1876

State legislatures across the South pass the first wave of discriminatory "Jim Crow" laws. *See p. 9.*

1877

President Rutherford B. Hayes orders federal troops out of the South, bringing the Reconstruction era to a close. *See p. 9.*

1895

Booker T. Washington delivers his "Atlanta Compromise" speech to a white audience at the Cotton States and International Exposition. *See p. 21.*

1896

In *Plessy v. Ferguson,* the U.S. Supreme Court rules that state laws in the South that require segregation of schools, passenger trains, and other facilities are constitutional. *See p. 9.*

1903

W.E.B. Du Bois publishes *The Souls of Black Folk.*

1905

Black civil rights leaders collectively known as the Niagara Movement meet on the Canadian side of Niagara Falls. *See p. 22.*

1909

The National Association for the Advancement of Colored People (NAACP) is founded. *See p. 22.*

1910

The civil rights organization National Urban League (NUL) is founded. *See p. 22.*

The NAACP literary magazine *The Crisis* is founded. *See p. 37.*

1914

World War I begins in Europe. *See p. 14.*

Marcus Garvey founds his Universal Negro Improvement Association (UNIA) in Jamaica. *See p. 32.*

1915

The "Great Migration" of Southern blacks to Northern cities intensifies, bringing tens of thousands of African-American workers to the industrial North. *See p. 13.*

1916

James Weldon Johnson is named field secretary of the National Association for the Advancement of Colored People.

1917

The United States enters World War I. *See p. 14.*

Three one-act plays featuring all-black casts—*The Rider of Dreams, Simon the Cyrenean*, and *Granny Maumee*—are performed at the Provincetown Playhouse in New York City.

More than 8,000 African Americans gather in New York City on July 28 to participate in a "Silent Protest" against white violence against blacks. *See p. 28.*

1919

American troops return home after the Allied victory in World War I. *See p. 16.*

Race riots collectively known as the "Red Summer" explode in more than twenty cities across the United States. *See p. 16.*

Claude McKay's famous poem "If We Must Die" is published. *See p. 41.*

The National Prohibition Enforcement Act (also known as the Volstead Act) is passed, ushering in a thirteen-year period when the sale of virtually all alcoholic beverages is prohibited in the United States.

1920

National Prohibition takes effect.

Marcus Garvey holds his First International Convention of the Negro Peoples of the World in New York City. *See p. 32.*

Membership in Marcus Garvey's UNIA surpasses one million members. *See p. 33.*

Playwright Eugene O'Neill casts black actor Charles Gilpin as the star of his new play *The Emperor Jones*. *See p. 62.*

Filmmaker Oscar Micheaux releases *Within Our Gates,* a defiant response to D.W. Griffith's racist movie *Birth of a Nation.*

James Weldon Johnson becomes executive secretary of the NAACP.

1921

Langston Hughes publishes his first poem, "The Negro Speaks of Rivers," in *The Crisis.* See p. 41.

Shuffle Along, a jazz musical written, composed, and performed by African Americans, becomes a smash hit in New York City. See p. 59.

1922

Duke Ellington moves to New York City.

Claude McKay's poetry collection *Harlem Shadows* is published. See p. 41.

James Weldon Johnson's influential *Book of American Negro Poetry* is published. See p. 41.

The National Urban League magazine *Opportunity* is founded. See p. 37.

The Harmon Foundation, an important philanthropical organization for Harlem Renaissance writers and artists, is founded.

1923

Jean Toomer's novel *Cane* is published to unanimous critical acclaim. See p. 43.

The African-American musical *Runnin' Wild* introduces the Charleston dance to America. See p. 62.

Blues singer Bessie Smith begins performing in New York City and launches her recording career with "Downhearted Blues."

The Cotton Club opens in Harlem. See p. 66.

1924

Jessie Redmon Fauset publishes her first novel, *There Is Confusion.* See p. 43.

Paul Robeson becomes America's newest stage star in Eugene O'Neill's *All God's Chillun Got Wings* and *The Emperor Jones.* See p. 63.

Walter Francis White's *The Fire in the Flint* is released. See p. 43.

Josephine Baker becomes an international star on the strength of her performance in *Chocolate Dandies.* See p. 62.

Painter Aaron Douglas arrives in Harlem and begins studying under Rinold Weiss.

Louis Armstrong makes his first extended stay in New York, playing with the Fletcher Henderson Orchestra.

1925

A special issue of *Survey Graphic* devoted to Harlem and its writers and artists hits American newsstands in March. An expanded version of the issue, edited by Alain

Locke, is released several months later as the book-length *The New Negro: An Interpretation*. *See p. 45.*

Countee Cullen's first volume of poetry, *Color*, is published.

Garland Anderson's play *Appearances* debuts on Broadway.

Paul Robeson sings in concert for the first time in New York City, launching a hugely successful singing career.

1926

The Weary Blues, Langston Hughes's first collection of poetry, is published. *See p. 50.*

The Savoy Ballroom opens in Harlem. *See p. 67.*

Carl Van Vechten's controversial novel *Nigger Heaven* becomes a bestseller. *See p. 46.*

Langston Hughes's influential essay "The Negro Artist and the Racial Mountain" appears in *The Nation*. *See p. 50.*

Editor Wallace Thurman releases the first and only issue of the radical literary magazine *Fire!! See p. 51.*

The Harmon Foundation holds the first of its annual exhibitions of paintings and sculptures by African-American artists at the Harlem branch of the New York Public Library. *See p. 69.*

1927

Langston Hughes publishes his second collection of poetry, *Fine Clothes to the Jew.*

God's Trombones, a series of traditional black sermons set to verse by James Weldon Johnson and illustrated by Aaron Douglas, is published. *See p. 52.*

The Duke Ellington Orchestra begins a four-year stint as the house band at the Cotton Club. *See p. 66.*

Marcus Garvey is deported back to Jamaica. *See p. 33.*

1928

Nella Larsen publishes her first novel, *Quicksand. See p. 53.*

Claude McKay's novel *Home to Harlem* becomes the first bestseller written by a black author in U.S. history. *See p. 54.*

Jazz legend Jelly Roll Morton leaves Chicago and settles in New York City.

Rudolph Fisher's novel *The Walls of Jericho* is published. *See p. 53.*

Zora Neale Hurston's essay "How It Feels To Be Colored Me" appears in *World Tomorrow. See p. 51.*

The W.E.B. Du Bois novel *Dark Princess* is released. *See p. 53.*

Paul Robeson makes "Ol' Man River" his signature song in a hit theatrical production of *Show Boat*.

1929

The Nella Larsen novel *Passing* is published. *See p. 53.*

Rope and Faggot, Walter F. White's explosive study of the history of lynching in America, is published.

The Wallace Thurman-William Jourdan Rapp play *Harlem* opens on Broadway. *See p. 63.*

A huge stock market crash in October brings the Jazz Age to a screeching halt and ushers in the Great Depression.

1930

James Weldon Johnson's epic history of Harlem, *Black Manhattan,* is published. *See p. 52.*

1931

Augusta Savage opens the Savage School of Arts and Crafts in Harlem.

The Scottsboro Nine are arrested in Alabama on false rape charges. *See p. 80.*

James Weldon Johnson leaves Harlem to take a position at Fisk University in Nashville.

1932

Wallace Thurman publishes his satirical novel *Infants of the Spring.* *See p. 54.*

Sterling Brown's *Southern Road* poetry collection is published. *See p. 53.*

1933

Jessie Redmon Fauset's last novel, *Comedy: American Style,* is published. *See p. 53.*

James Weldon Johnson publishes his autobiography, *Along This Way.*

The Twenty-First Amendment to the U.S. Constitution, which ends Prohibition, is ratified.

1934

Zora Neale Hurston's first novel, *Jonah's Gourd Vine,* reaches American bookstores. *See p. 54.*

Langston Hughes publishes his short story collection *The Ways of White Folks.*

Aaron Douglas begins work on his epic *Aspects of Negro Life* murals for the Harlem branch of the New York Public Library. *See p. 69.*

W.E.B. Du Bois resigns from *The Crisis* and leaves New York City for Atlanta, Georgia. *See p. 78.*

1935

The Langston Hughes play *Mulatto* opens on Broadway.

A deadly and destructive riot breaks out in Harlem on March 19, shattering the illusion of Harlem as an idyllic paradise for African Americans. *See p. 82.*

1937

Their Eyes Were Watching God, Zora Neale Hurston's best-known novel, is published. *See p. 54.*

1940

Langston Hughes publishes his autobiography, *The Big Sea.*

SOURCES FOR FURTHER STUDY

Harlem Renaissance: A Multimedia Resource. Available online at http://www.jcu.edu/harlem/index.html. This Internet site, created and maintained at John Carroll University, features a wide range of audio, video, and text materials that touch on a wide assortment of Harlem Renaissance topics, including literature, religion, education, art, and political activism.

Hill, Laban Carrick. *Harlem Stomp! A Cultural History of the Harlem Renaissance.* New York: Little, Brown, 2004. This colorful, heavily illustrated history of the Harlem Renaissance era is written especially for juvenile audiences.

Jabbar, Kareem Abdul, with Raymond Obstfeld. *On the Shoulders of Giants: My Journey Through the Harlem Renaissance.* New York: Simon and Schuster, 2007. NBA basketball legend Kareem Abdul Jabbar blends memoir and history together in this entertaining book. Much of the book is devoted to a warm retelling of the triumphs of the Harlem Renaissance era, but the author also includes numerous anecdotes about his own youthful experiences and memories of New York City in the 1940s and 1950s.

Lewis, David Levering. *The Portable Harlem Renaissance Reader.* New York: Viking Press, 1994. The selections in this anthology of poetry, short stories, essays, and novel excerpts highlight all of the major writers of the Harlem Renaissance, including such leading figures as Langston Hughes, Claude McKay, Zora Neale Hurston, and James Weldon Johnson. The book also features interesting introductory notes for many of the pieces, as well as brief but valuable biographies of all featured writers.

Locke, Alain, ed. *The New Negro: Voices of the Harlem Renaissance.* New York: Touchstone, 1999. This reprint of the famous book published at the height of the Harlem Renaissance features contributions from Langston Hughes, Countee Cullen, and many other African-American writers. It also includes an introduction by Arnold Rampersad, a noted Harlem Renaissance scholar.

Wilson, Sondra Kathryn, ed. The Crisis *Reader: Stories, Poetry and Essays from the N.A.A.C.P.'s* Crisis Magazine. New York: Modern Library, 1999.

Wilson, Sondra Kathryn, ed. The Opportunity *Reader: Stories, Poetry and Essays from the Urban League's* Opportunity Magazine. New York: Modern Library, 1999. These two books provide histories of the two leading black magazines of the Harlem Renaissance. Both titles feature a wealth of reprinted essays, poems, and stories by many of the leading African-American writers of the era.

BIBLIOGRAPHY

Books and Periodicals

Anderson, Paul Allen. *Deep River: Music and Memory in Harlem Renaissance Thought.* Durham, NC: Duke University Press, 2001.

Bontemps, Arna, ed. *The Harlem Renaissance Remembered: Essays.* New York: Dodd, Mead, 1972.

Bloom, Harold, ed. *Black American Poets and Dramatists of the Harlem Renaissance.* New York: Chelsea House, 1996.

Boyd, Herb, ed. *The Harlem Reader: A Celebration of New York's Most Famous Neighborhood, From the Renaissance Years to the 21st Century.* New York: Three Rivers Press, 2003.

Boyle, Kevin. *Arc of Justice: A Saga of Race, Civil Rights, and Murder in the Jazz Age.* New York: Henry Holt, 2004.

Calloway, Cab, and Bryant Rollins. *Of Minnie the Moocher and Me.* New York: Crowell, 1976.

Campbell, Mary Schmidt, ed. *Harlem Renaissance: Art of Black America.* New York: Abrams, 1994.

Fabre, Geneviève, and Michael Feith. *Temples for Tomorrow: Looking Back at the Harlem Renaissance.* Bloomington: Indiana University Press, 2001.

Franklin, John Hope, and Alfred Moss, Jr. *From Slavery to Freedom: A History of African Americans.* 8th ed. New York: Knopf, 2000.

Gregory, James N. *The Southern Diaspora: How the Great Migrations of Black and White Southerners Transformed America.* Chapel Hill: University of North Carolina Press, 2007.

Haskins, James. *Black Theater in America.* New York: Crowell, 1982.

Huggins, Nathan Irvin, ed. *Voices from the Harlem Renaissance.* New York: Oxford University Press, 1995.

Hughes, Langston. *The Big Sea: An Autobiography.* New York: Hill and Wang, 1993.

Hurston, Zora Neale. *Folklore, Memoirs, and Other Writings: Zora Neale Hurston.* Edited by Cheryl A. Wall. New York: Library of America, 1995.

Hutchinson, George. *The Harlem Renaissance in Black and White.* Cambridge, MA: Belknap Press of Harvard University, 1995.

Kellner, Bruce. *Harlem Renaissance: A Historical Dictionary for the Era.* New York: Methuen, 1987.

Kirschke, Amy H. "Oh Africa! The Influence of African Art during the Harlem Renaissance." In *Temples for Tomorrow: Looking Back at the Harlem Renaissance.* Edited by Geneviève Fabre and Michael Feith. Bloomington: Indiana University Press, 2001.

Lewis, David Levering. "Harlem Renaissance." *Encyclopedia of African-American Culture and History.* 5 vols. New York: Macmillan, 1996.

Lewis, David Levering. *The Portable Harlem Renaissance Reader.* New York: Viking Press, 1994.

Lewis, David Levering. *When Harlem Was in Vogue.* New York: Knopf, 1981.

Locke, Alain. *The New Negro: Voices of the Harlem Renaissance.* 1925. New York: Touchstone, 1997.

Marks, Carole, and Diana Edkins. *The Power of Pride: Stylemakers and Rulebreakers of the Harlem Renaissance.* New York: Crown, 1999.

Michlin, Monica. "Langston Hughes's Blues." In *Temples for Tomorrow: Looking Back at the Harlem Renaissance.* Edited by Geneviève Fabre and Michael Feith. Bloomington: Indiana University Press, 2001.

Osofsky, Gilbert. *Harlem: The Making of a Ghetto: Negro New York, 1890-1930.* New York: Harper & Row, 1966.

Spencer, Jon Michael. *The New Negroes and Their Music: The Success of the Harlem Renaissance.* Knoxville: University of Tennessee Press, 1997.

Sterling, Dorothy, ed. *Trouble They Seen: The Story of Reconstruction in the Words of African Americans.* New York: Da Capo Press, 1994.

Stovall, Tyler. *Paris Noir: African Americans in the City of Light.* New York: Houghton Mifflin, 1996.

Stuart, Andrea. "The Harlem Renaissance in the Twenties Produced a Wealth of Black Talent. But What was Its Legacy and Who Did It Really Benefit?" *New Statesman (1996),* June 27, 1997.

Tillery, Tyrone. "Claude McKay" In *Harlem Speaks: A Living History of the Harlem Renaissance.* Edited by Cary D. Wintz. Naperville, IL: Sourcebooks, 2007.

Wagner, Jean. *Black Poets of the United States: From Paul Laurence Dunbar to Langston Hughes.* Urbana, IL: University of Illinois Press, 1973.

Watson, Steven. *The Harlem Renaissance: Hub of African-American Culture, 1920-1930.*

Williams, Lloyd A., and Voza W. Rivers. *Forever Harlem: Celebrating America's Most Diverse Community.* New York: Spotlight Press, 2006.

Wintz, Cary D. *Black Culture and the Harlem Renaissance.* Houston: Rice University Press, 1988.

Wintz, Cary D., ed. *Harlem Speaks: A Living History of the Harlem Renaissance.* Naperville, IL: Sourcebooks, 2007.

Wintz, Cary D., ed. *Remembering the Harlem Renaissance.* Vol. 5 of *The Harlem Renaissance, 1920-1940* (7 vols.). New York: Garland, 1996.

Online

"Guide to Harlem Renaissance Materials." Available online at the Library of Congress, www.loc.gov/rr/program/bib/harlem/harlem.html (accessed September 2007).

"Harlem, 1900-1940: An African American Community." Available online at the Schomburg Center for Research in Black Culture, New York Public Library, www.si.umich.edu/CHICO/Harlem/Index.html (accessed September 2007).

Powell, Richard, and Jeffrey Stewart. "Online NewsHour Forum: Harlem Renaissance." Available online at PBS, *Online NewsHour,* www.pbs.org/newshour, February 20, 1998 (accessed September 2007).

"Rhapsodies in Black: The Art of the Harlem Renaissance." Available online at the Institute of International Visual Arts, www.iniva.org/harlem/index2.html (accessed September 2007).

DVD and VHS

Against the Odds: The Artists of the Harlem Renaissance. DVD. Public Broadcasting System (PBS), 1993.

Harlem Renaissance: Fats Waller, Duke Ellington, Count Basie, Nat King Cole. DVD. Kultur, 2004.

Jazz: A Film by Ken Burns. 10 episodes. VHS. Public Broadcasting System (PBS), 2001.

PHOTO CREDITS

INDEX